$19.95
47335
7/18

D1369700

Greg Saltyman

Public-Sector Bargaining

Public-Sector Bargaining

A Policy Reappraisal

Myron Lieberman

LexingtonBooks
D.C. Heath and Company
Lexington, Massachusetts
Toronto

Library of Congress Cataloging in Publication Data

Lieberman, Myron,   1919-
   Public-sector bargaining.

   Bibliography: p.
   Includes index.
   1. Collective bargaining—State government employees—United States.
2. Collective bargaining—Local officials and employees—United States.
I. Title.
HD8005.6.U5L53   331.89'04135'0000973   80-8426
ISBN 0-669-04110-6

Copyright © 1980 by D.C. Heath and Company

All rights reserved. No part of this publication may be reproduced or transmitted in any form or by any means, electronic or mechanical, including photocopy, recording, or any information storage or retrieval system, without permission in writing from the publisher.

Second printing, May 1981

Published simultaneously in Canada

Printed in the United States of America

International Standard Book Number: 0-669-04110-6

Library of Congress Catalog Card Number: 80-8426

*This book is dedicated to Max Weiner, and
to the memory of our friend and
colleague, Benjamin Rosner*

Contents

List of Tables

Preface

Although the following analysis must stand or fall on its merits, an author's experience and point of view may provide helpful clues to readers. For this reason, some comment on these matters may be appropriate.

My own experience with public-sector bargaining has been largely in public education. Whether my views on public-sector bargaining would be different if my experience had been in fields outside of education is perhaps best left to others to say. In any event, my activities related to public-sector bargaining extend over a thirty-year period, beginning with membership in the St. Paul Federation of Teachers in 1948-1949. When I left the St. Paul public schools to pursue a doctoral program, I became a charter member of the American Federation of Teachers (AFT) Local 1055 at the University of Illinois. In 1956 my first book (*Education as a Profession*) predicted and supported the advent of collective bargaining in public education.

Publication of *Education as a Profession* was followed by almost two decades of close involvement with the National Education Association (NEA) and the AFT. In 1962 I was an active candidate for president of the AFT and received just over a third of the convention votes for that office. From 1972 to 1974 I directed a program for training teacher-organization leaders on public-policy issues. This program was endorsed by both the NEA and the AFT, and both organizations officially expressed approval of my initiation and direction of the program. During this period I was a member of both organizations and an elected delegate to the national conventions of both. These were only a few of my activities in or related to public-sector unions from 1956 to 1975. After 1975 my organizational activities declined, but my published works continued to advocate or assume the legitimacy of public-sector bargaining until February 1979, when I wrote an article questioning some of the arguments commonly used to justify public-sector bargaining.

No one incident or development triggered my change of views concerning the desirability of public-sector bargaining. Certainly, being employed by school boards as a negotiator did not have this effect; although I was employed in this capacity from 1967 to 1978 and was frequently critical of specific provisions in state bargaining laws, I did not challenge the legitimacy of public-sector bargaining during this time. In fact, my advocacy of public-sector bargaining during this period was as strong as or stronger than it had been at any time previously. Nevertheless it became increasingly clear to me in the late 1970s that certain arguments against public-sector bargaining had not been considered, or considered fully, in the past. One need only compare the issues discussed in this book with those discussed in my previous books (especially *Collective Negotiations for*

Teachers, which I coauthored in 1966) to appreciate the fact that earlier analyses neglected several crucial issues pertaining to the desirability of public-sector bargaining. Consideration of these issues led to a reassessment of others that had previously been regarded as settled. As John Dewey once observed, if people start thinking, there is no way to predict what the outcome will be.

Vilfredo Pareto pointed out that men easily convert their interests into convictions. It is therefore understandable why my change of views should be regarded in some quarters as merely the adoption of an ideology that serves my economic interests. This is a legitimate issue, especially since my analysis raises similar issues with respect to others involved in public-sector bargaining. I certainly do not claim a higher moral posture than those who differ with me on the issues discussed in this book; however, neither am I about to concede that my analysis is only self-serving propaganda. Although I supported public-sector bargaining for twelve years, while employed as a management negotiator, let me make a few additional observations and leave the matter to the judgment of the reader.

The first is that the most successful management representatives in collective bargaining do not challenge the institution of collective bargaining itself. As a matter of fact, the most successful management negotiators in both public and private employment emphasize avoidance of any actions or statements that can be characterized as "union-busting"; needless to say, any serious challenge to public-sector bargaining is likely to be characterized as "union-busting" by public-sector unions.

Finally, the notion that criticisms of public-sector bargaining enhance one's position or employment opportunities with public employers is misleading. Undoubtedly most public employers welcome criticisms of public-sector bargaining. Nevertheless, such criticism does not translate into enhanced employment opportunities for the critic. Public employers who welcome criticisms of public-sector bargaining do not necessarily want to employ the critic. Why employ someone who is waving a red flag at the union before even stepping foot in the community? In any case, I hope that the arguments in this book will be understood and evaluated on their merits, and that the same criteria will be applied to the arguments of others.

Myron Lieberman
904 Encina Avenue
Modesto, CA 95354

Acknowledgments

I began writing this reappraisal on 22 March 1980 and completed it in late August of 1980. By my personal standards, at least, this was a relatively short period of time. Only the cooperation and assistance of several people made this possible. Among those due a special word of appreciation are Professor Robert Holtzman of Temple University; John Barth, Research Director, Public Service Research Council; Professor Paul F. Gearhart, Case-Western Reserve University; Professor Peter Hennessy, Queen's University, Kingston, Ontario; Jerome Lefkowitz, Deputy Director, New York State Public Employment Relations Board; and Robert D. Helsby, Director of the Public Employment Relations Service, Albany, New York. It would be most unfair to attribute any position in this study to any of these individuals, at least on the basis of what is said here.

I would also like to express my appreciation to the Institute of Industrial Relations at the University of California at Berkeley, which provided full access to its resources. Needless to say, I am solely responsible for the content of this study.

Introduction

In the past twenty years, the entire context of public-sector bargaining has changed drastically. For instance, the legislatures that have not enacted public-employee bargaining laws are under increasing pressure to do so. When no state or a very few had enacted such legislation, the proponents of public-sector bargaining carried a much heavier burden in persuading legislatures to enact it. Furthermore, the public employees in nonbargaining states are now more easily persuaded that they are the victims of discrimination. This situation did not arise in the early 1960s, when relatively few public employees had bargaining rights. At that time public employees could not argue, as they can today, that most states had enacted such legislation. Of course, this is not really a logical argument for enactment, any more than the nonexistence of such legislation is a valid argument for its nonenactment. Nevertheless, legislators are often interested in and influenced by the way other legislatures have dealt with a problem. A legislator who does not know much about bargaining, who discovers that most states have enacted bargaining legislation, who has politically influential constituents according it high legislative priority, and who regards the arguments for enactment plausible and the contrary arguments rather weak is a good prospect to support such legislation.

Second, public-sector bargaining has led to an enormous increase in the membership, resources, and political influence of public-sector unions. What has been done, therefore, cannot be so easily undone. A private individual may come to regard earlier support for public-sector bargaining as a mistake. It is much more difficult for a political leader to do so. Apart from public embarrassment from changing positions, the presence of politically powerful public-sector unions is not conducive to either this thought process or its public expression.

Another change is attitudinal. Twenty years ago the phrase "no contract, no work" was exceptional in the public sector. Neither the leaders nor the rank-and-file members of public-employee organizations embraced the concept. Today, however, the concept has been widely adopted by many public employees, and a strong presumption of its legitimacy is part of the context of public-sector bargaining.

These changes in the context of public-employment relations reflect a new conventional wisdom about these relations. This study is a critique of this new conventional wisdom. Like any such critique, it is not likely to be favorably received by the interests it proposes to unsettle. These interests extend far beyond public employees and public-employee unions. They include, but are not limited to, the impartial third-party industry, the labor-relations community in higher education, and a significant number of elected officials and representatives of public management. For many of these participants in public-sector bargaining, evidence about it is useful only to support positions held independently of the evidence. Probably no amount of evidence could ever persuade the leadership of public-sector unions that public-sector bargaining is undesirable public policy, just as no evidence could convince some public officials that any limitation on their rights to act unilaterally in personnel matters is desirable. Nonetheless, for those not committed to a position regardless of the evidence, there is now a great deal of relevant evidence that was not available when most state bargaining laws were enacted. The relevance is to the public-policy desirability of public-sector bargaining; what was believed or speculated in the 1960s can now be tested against our actual experience with the process. In part, therefore, this analysis is an effort to review the rationale for public sector bargaining in the light of our twenty-year experience with it.

Although a significant portion of this analysis is devoted to interest-group influence on public-sector labor relations, the analysis does not assume that union leaders are more motivated by self-interest than any other group in our society. As a matter of fact, some critics of public-sector bargaining have misled themselves as well as others by their tunnel vision on this issue. They have tended to ignore the mini-industries and satellite occupations that have emerged or prospered as a result of public-sector bargaining and the role these entities play not only in public-sector bargaining itself but in public and legislative attitudes toward it. Thus the impartial third-party industry (mediators, arbitrators, and fact-finders) has flourished as never before as a vast new market (public employment) has opened up for its services. The same can be said about a growing number of college professors who moonlight as impartial third parties and bureaucrats in the state agencies whose *raison d'être* is to regulate public-sector bargaining. Last, but not least, public officials themselves often have a stake in public-sector bargaining that is not fully revealed to the communities they serve.

These are some of the leading groups that reinforce the belief in the desirability or the inevitability of public-sector bargaining. In the face of such widespread opposition, an argument that it is neither risks the appearance of fatuousness. My concern here, however, is not that particular risk but the exclusive focus on the union role in establishing, maintaining, and expanding public-sector bargaining. This narrow focus exaggerates union power and shields the role of other important groups from critical scrutiny. The scrutiny of these other groups in this book is decidedly inadequate, but an effort has been made to consider their role, even if it is not discussed in detail.

Some editorial and analytical problems recur throughout this book. For various reasons, the book is limited to state and local public employment, even though some of the analysis applies to the federal sector. Rather than continually qualifying the analysis to ensure that its application to the federal sector is correct, I have omitted any discussion of collective bargaining in the federal sector. It should be understood, therefore, that such terms as *public-sector bargaining*, *public-employee union*, and *public employer* in this book denote state governments and public employers created by state governments, such as cities and school boards. Although a great deal of the analysis does apply to federal employment, the analysis of federal-sector bargaining is left to others.

I should also clarify a semantic problem that may otherwise be troublesome. The terms *public-employee unions*, *public-sector unions*, and *public-sector bargaining* are sometimes used synonymously, even though, strictly speaking, these terms refer to different things. For instance, *public-sector bargaining* refers to a process, whereas *public-sector unions* refers to organizations. Technically, there could be an increase in either the process or the organizations involved in it without any increase or decrease in the other. Thus union membership might be increasing while the number of bargaining units represented by the union is decreasing. It would also be possible for a union with declining membership to increase its bargaining activities. A substantial increase in bargaining may be achieved by a single union or by a multiplicity of unions whose membership fluctuates widely. In other words, there is no simple, straightforward relationship between a change in the process and a change in the organizations.

As a practical matter, however, an increase in bargaining usually leads to an increase in union membership and resources, and vice versa. For this reason, it seemed appropriate to use *public-sector union* to include public-sector bargaining, or vice versa, when my purpose was to discuss a complex of events that included both the organizations and the process. Needless to say, where it is important to maintain the distinction, I have tried to do so.

Initial clarification of several other frequently used terms seems desirable. By *public policy*, I mean a policy adopted by a public body. Thus state statutes, municipal ordinances, and school-board policies are all public policies, as the phrase is used here. Regulations promulgated by public administrators but not requiring any legislative approval would normally be included also.

Similarly, the term *political issue* denotes controversy, actual or potential, over public policy as defined. Even when public officials are elected on a nonpartisan ballot, the policies they legislate are still political issues, as the term is used here. Thus the term is not used in a perjorative sense, or to denote only issues involving political parties or candidates. Any time a public agency deals with a controversial policy, that policy is a political issue in this study.

Throughout this book it was necessary to refer to the state agencies that administer public-sector labor relations. These state agencies are responsible for making unit determinations, supervising representation and election procedures, conducting hearings on charges of unfair labor practices, and (usually) administering the impasse procedures prescribed by statute. A common title for such an agency is *public employment relations board* (PERB). I use the acronym PERB to refer to such a board, even if the acronym does not reflect the official title in many states.

Some unions, such as the National Education Association and the Service Employees International Union (AFL-CIO), represent employees in both the public and private sectors. The term *public-sector union* is used in this book to denote any union active in the public sector, whether or not it represents only public employees. Here again, however, I have tried to avoid making any statement that is invalid as a result of failure to draw the distinction between unions that enroll only public employees and unions that enroll both private and public employees.

One other usage should be noted. The term *bargainist* is used to denote a supporter of public-sector bargaining; the term *antibargainist* is used to denote opponents of such bargaining. Obviously, there are many significant differences within and between these groups; however, a simple term to denote each broad group is useful for certain purposes.

As previously noted, I regard collective bargaining in the public sector as undesirable public policy. In my opinion, the reasons for thinking so will be more widely discussed and accepted in the 1980s than they have been at any time in the past. In fact, my belief that these reasons have not been articulated adequately in legislatures, academic institutions, media, professional organizations and journals, and among the public at large underlies this effort to do so.

It also seems safe to predict that increasing political and academic attention to public-sector bargaining will be accompanied by increased judicial scrutiny of it. As is or was the case with racial segregation, abortion, reapportionment, rights of the indigent, government secrecy, sex discrimination, and many other leading political issues, public-sector bargaining also raises some important constitutional issues. The view that such bargaining should be declared unconstitutional (as violative of the fifth and fourteenth amendments to the U.S. Constitution) is shared by a growing number of lawyers; several are already litigating the issue in various forums. Unquestionably, the U.S. Supreme Court will eventually have to grapple with the underlying issues. My belief that public-sector bargaining is headed or decline is not predicated upon the expectation of a Supreme Court decision prohibiting it, but such a development is more than a remote possibility.

To be sure, an immediate decline of public-sector bargaining is an unlikely development. In the early 1980s such bargaining may even continue to grow, especially where inflation is particularly damaging to public employees. Nevertheless, public-sector bargaining will encounter growing opposition on the legislative, political, and judicial fronts, such that it is unlikely to maintain its present influence, let alone increase it.

In making this argument, I have not always documented the basis for certain legal principles of collective bargaining asserted in the text. Such documentation will virtually always be available in one or both of two exceptionally comprehensive and scholarly publications, which include extensive bibliographies and perceptive discussions of policy and legal issues. The first, which covers collective bargaining in the private sector, is Robert A. Gorman, *Basic Text on Labor Law, Unionization and Collective Bargaining* (St. Paul: West Publishing Co., 1976). The other, which is devoted to public-sector bargaining, is Harry T. Edwards, R. Theodore Clark, Jr., and Charles B. Craver, *Labor Relations Law in the Public Sector* (Indianapolis: Bobbs-Merrill, 1979). Partly because these resources are readily available, I have not documented many statements that might be questioned by interested readers. Of course, any errors in stating the legal or the factual situation are solely my responsibility.

The argument itself is developed as follows. Chapter 1 presents an overview of the rise and present status of public-sector bargaining. Although some attention is paid to rationale, the main emphasis is upon the tremendous growth of public-sector unions: the number of public employees, membership in public-employee unions, the state jurisdictions involved, the resources of public-sector unions, and so on. Chapter 2 discusses the early debate on public-sector bargaining; as we shall see, many of the crucial issues pertaining to public-sector bargaining were not even raised, let alone discussed, in this early debate. Chapter 3 discusses the argument that public employees should have collective-bargaining rights as a matter of procedural equity with private-sector employees. Chapter 4 raises several policy issues growing out of the political dimension to public-sector bargaining. Chapter 5 continues this discussion by analyzing contract administration in the light of the political dimension to public-sector bargaining. The major issue raised is whether binding arbitration of grievances does in fact result in the adoption of public policies by parties who are not politically accountable to the electorate.

Chapter 6 deals with constitutional issues, which have been neglected but are rapidly emerging as major problems in public-sector bargaining. This chapter, as much as any, delineates several basic differences between public- and private-sector employment—differences largely overlooked in the past two decades. In chapter 7 the analysis deals with a remarkable omission in the debate over public-sector bargaining since its inception—the absence of critical attention to the costs of the process. The concluding chapter then suggests some needed reforms in the state bargaining statutes. These suggestions are based on the view that much can be done to improve these statutes apart from their repeal, which is an unlikely development.

As will be evident, the analysis in this book does not rely upon or cite empirical studies to any great extent. The main reason is that empirical confirmation of most major points would belabor the obvious. Any reasonably intelligent adult who understands the basic dynamics of collective bargaining should be able to understand the analysis of public-sector bargaining in this book. The basic arguments are simple and fundamental, and nothing is gained by dressing them up in esoteric language or citing studies that only confirm the obvious.

**Public-Sector
Bargaining**

1 The Rise of Public-Sector Bargaining

This chapter provides an overview of public-sector bargaining. The basic data set forth are not precise, but they should suffice for their intended purpose, which is to show the tremendous expansion of public-sector bargaining from 1960 to 1980. Before analyzing the data, however, it would be helpful to review the statistics on union membership in the private sector. These statistics indicate some factors that affect unionization in the public as well as in the private sector.

Table 1-1 provides an overview of U.S. union membership since 1930. It shows that private-sector membership remained fairly stable from 1930 to 1936, a period that included the worst depression this nation has ever experienced. Within this six-year period, private-sector-union membership as a percentage of the total private-sector labor force never changed more than 0.8 percent in any one year. Membership increased dramatically in the late 1930s as a result of the enactment of the National Labor Relations Act (NLRA), which provided federal protections for private-sector unions and collective bargaining. Membership also increased substantially during World War II, mainly as a result of the policies of the War Labor Board (WLB). This federal agency was established to deal with labor-management problems during the war. In its approach to these problems, the WLB supported union-security provisions that increased union membership. Membership continued to increase until 1953, reaching a peak of 25.5 percent of the entire labor force in that year. Since then, union membership in absolute numbers has remained rather constant, but it has steadily declined as a percent of the total private-sector labor force. In fact, expressed as a percent of the labor force, union membership in the private sector sank to 16.2 percent in 1978, the lowest figure since 1940.

Although it shows that membership in public-sector unions quadrupled from 1956 to 1978, table 1-1 vastly understates the actual increase. The reason is that the figures in table 1-1 do not include members of public-employee associations, although many of these associations are unions. The Bureau of Labor Statistics (BLS) defines *union* as a public-employee organization that is affiliated with the AFL-CIO and has not functioned as a professional association. An *association* is defined as an employee organization that is not affiliated with the AFL-CIO and has functioned as a professional association. The distinction is not very useful or helpful.

Table 1-1
U.S. Union Membership, 1930-1978

Year	Total Work Force	Private-Sector Membership	Percent of Work Force	Public-Sector Membership	Percent of Work Force
1930	50,080,000	3,401,000	6.8	—	—
1931	50,680,000	3,310,000	6.5	—	—
1932	51,250,000	3,050,000	6.0	—	—
1933	51,840,000	2,689,000	5.2	—	—
1934	52,490,000	3,088,000	5.9	—	—
1935	53,140,000	3,584,000	6.7	—	—
1936	53,740,000	3,989,000	7.4	—	—
1937	54,320,000	7,001,000	12.9	—	—
1938	54,950,000	8,034,000	14.6	—	—
1939	55,600,000	8,763,000	15.8	—	—
1940	56,180,000	8,717,000	15.5	—	—
1941	57,530,000	10,201,000	17.7	—	—
1942	60,380,000	10,380,000	17.2	—	—
1943	64,560,000	13,213,000	20.5	—	—
1944	66,040,000	14,146,000	21.4	—	—
1945	65,300,000	14,322,000	21.9	—	—
1946	60,970,000	14,395,000	23.6	—	—
1947	61,758,000	14,787,000	23.9	—	—
1948	62,080,000	14,319,000	23.1	—	—
1949	62,903,000	14,282,000	22.7	—	—
1950	63,858,000	14,267,000	22.3	—	—
1951	65,117,000	15,946,000	24.5	—	—
1952	65,730,000	15,892,000	24.2	—	—
1953	66,560,000	16,948,000	25.5	—	—
1954	66,993,000	17,022,000	25.4	—	—
1955	68,077,000	16,802,000	24.7	—	—
1956[a]	69,409,000	16,575,000	23.9	915,000	1.3
1958	70,275,000	15,994,000	22.7	1,035,000	1.5
1960	72,142,000	15,979,000	22.1	1,070,000	1.5
1962	73,442,000	15,361,000	20.9	1,225,000	1.7
1964	75,830,000	15,388,000	20.3	1,453,000	1.9
1966	78,893,000	16,223,000	20.5	1,717,000	2.2
1968	82,272,000	16,761,000	20.4	2,155,000	2.6
1970	85,903,000	17,063,000	19.9	2,318,000	2.7
1972	88,991,000	16,975,000	19.1	2,460,000	2.7
1974	93,240,000	17,279,000	18.5	2,920,000	3.1
1976	96,917,000	16,622,000	17.1	3,012,000	3.1
1978	102,537,000	16,613,000	16.2	3,625,000	3.5

Association Membership in Public Sector

Year	Membership	Percent of Total Work Force
1968[b]	1,702,000	2.1
1970	1,762,000	2.1
1972	2,060,000	2.3
1974	2,425,000	2.6
1976	2,840,000	2.9
1978	2,394,000	2.3

Source: Statistics compiled from Bureau of Labor Statistics, U.S. Department of Labor materials; primarily the *Directory of National Unions and Employee Associations*, 1973 and 1975.

[a]Statistics for public-sector unions kept only since 1956 and available only at two-year intervals.

[b]Statistics for public-sector associations only kept since 1968 and only available at two year intervals.

Many associations as defined by the BLS are de facto unions engaged in bargaining, but for legal, tactical, or historical reasons, they avoid the labels "union" and "collective bargaining."

To illustrate, the National Education Association (NEA) has some local affiliates that bargain de jure, some that bargain de facto while referred to as "associations," and some that engage in a process not called bargaining but that culminates in a written agreement. It also has affiliates that make no effort to bargain. Nevertheless, although most NEA affiliates bargain collectively, all are categorized as associations by the BLS. Clearly, however, if one goes by the realities instead of the labels, most associations of public employees, as the BLS uses the term, are unions engaged in collective bargaining.

Table 1-2 is therefore a much more accurate indication of government union membership from 1970 to 1978; it suggests that membership in state and local public-sector unions increased 1.85 million during this eight-year period alone. The increase in the proportion of public-sector employees in unions is all the more remarkable since the state and local government work force increased by almost 3 million employees during this period. In all areas of public employment, however, the unions were organizing a larger and larger share of work force that was itself increasing in size. By any standards, public-sector unions were a growth industry in the 1960s and 1970s.

The changing patterns of union membership are matters of widespread discussion. There is no need to review the extensive literature on the subject here, except to point out that patterns of private- and public-sector-union membership are very similar in at least one crucial respect, to wit, the role of government. Just as the enactment of the NLRA and the support for union security by the WLB were key factors in the growth of private-sector unions, the supportive role of government has probably been the single most important factor associated with public-sector bargaining. Where states legalized public-sector bargaining, it increased dramatically, as did membership in public-sector unions. Where states opposed public-sector bargaining, it seldom emerged. And where states neither legalized nor prohibited public-sector bargaining, as in Ohio, public-sector bargaining emerged in an irregular but generally pro-bargaining pattern, at least outside the Sun Belt and mountain states. Note, however, that public-sector bargaining was (and is) not necessarily illegal in the absence of a statute legalizing it. Prior to a statutory enactment, the legal status of public-sector bargaining might have been unclear, or it might have been legal pursuant to judicial decisions that left many important issues unresolved. In any event, the enactment of a bargaining statute invariably results in a substantial increase in public-sector unionization and bargaining.

The spectacular growth of public-sector unions in especially evident in the membership figures for the three largest public-sector unions: the National Education Association (NEA), the American Federation of State, County, and Municipal Employees, AFL-CIO (AFSCME), and the

Table 1-2
Membership in Public-Sector Unions, 1970-1978
(Numbers in thousands)

	Total Government			Federal			State and Local		
Year	Membership	Employment	Percent Organized	Membership	Employment	Percent Organized	Membership	Employment	Percent Organized
1970	4,080	12,561	32.5	1,411	2,731	51.7	2,669	9,830	27.2
1972	4,520	13,340	33.9	1,394	2,684	51.9	3,126	10,656	29.3
1974	5,345	14,177	37.7	1,433	2,724	52.6	3,912	11,453	34.2
1976	5,852	14,948	39.1	1,334	2,733	48.8	4,518	12,215	37.0
1978	6,154	15,476	39.8	1,633	2,753	59.3	4,521	12,723	35.5

Source: U.S. Department of Labor, Bureau of Labor Statistics, Washington, D.C., 1980. Latest membership data are from *Directory of National Unions and Employee Associations*, table 16, to be published in summer 1980. Latest employment data are from *Employment and Earnings*, March 1979, table B-2.

American Federation of Teachers, AFL-CIO (AFT). As table 1-3 shows, their growth has been truly phenomenal during the past two decades.

Public-Sector Unions from a Government Perspective

To understand the growth of public-sector unions, one must look at more than the statistics on union membership. It is also necessary to consider the number and proportion of governments affected, the number of bargaining units and collective agreements, the total number of employees covered, and the impact of unionization on different categories of public employees. Table 1-4 provides an overview of several important dimensions of public-sector bargaining as of October 1977. It shows that the growth of public-sector unions has not been uniform among all types of public jurisdiction or among all categories of public employees. It is important to recognize these diversities as well as the enormous overall expansion of public-sector unionism.

Table 1-5 reveals the enormous diversity between states on the extent of employee organization. It shows that in 25 states, less than 40 percent of full-time employees were organized; in 26 states, 40 percent or more were organized. Tables 1-6 and 1-7 show the variations from two additional perspectives. Table 1-6 shows that school-district employees are most likely to be organized and that county-government employees are the least likely. Undoubtedly, these differences reflect to some extent different orientations among categories of public employees. Table 1-7 shows that firefighters and teachers are most likely to be organized whereas hospital and welfare workers are among the least likely to be organized.

Table 1-3
Membership in NEA, AFSCME, and AFT, 1960-1978

Year	NEA	AFSCME	AFT
1960	713,994	210,000	56,156
1962	812,497	220,000	70,821
1964	903,384	234,839	100,000
1966	986,113	281,277	125,000
1968	1,081,660	364,486	165,000
1970	1,100,155	444,479	205,323
1972	1,165,617	529,035	248,521
1974	1,470,212	648,160	444,000
1976	1,886,532	957,000	446,045
1978	1,696,469	1,020,000	500,000

Source: *NEA Handbook* (Washington, D.C.: National Education Association, 1979, p. 143; and Bureau of Labor Statistics, *Directory of National Unions and Employee Associations* (Washington, D.C.: Department of Labor, various editions).

Table 1-4

Summary of State and Local Government Labor-Management Relations, October 1977

Item	State and Local Governments	State Governments	Local Governments					
			Total	Counties	Municipalities	Townships	Special Districts	School Districts
Number of Governments	79,928	50	79,878	3,040	18,878	16,827	26,010	15,123
Governments with Labor Relations Policies, Total	13,094	41	13,053	665	2,383	981	763	8,261
By type of Policy:								
Collective negotiations only	5,523	6	5,517	303	971	424	313	3,506
Meet and confer discussions only	2,359	6	2,353	107	452	43	199	1,552
Both collective negotiations and meet and confer discussions	5,212	29	5,183	255	960	514	251	3,203
Total Employment, Full-time and Part-Time	12,765,146	3,490,853	9,274,293	1,761,242	2,623,271	360,763	401,880	4,127,137
Full-time Employees Only	9,861,426	2,676,910	7,184,516	1,492,666	2,068,724	217,503	327,233	3,078,390
By function:								
Education	4,552,488	759,442	3,793,046	288,999	330,610	95,634	—	3,077,803
Instructional staff	3,049,042	292,235	2,756,807	209,834	252,668	75,242	—	2,219,063
Other	1,503,446	467,207	1,036,239	79,165	77,942	20,392	—	858,740
Highways	541,111	255,668	285,443	126,731	126,851	27,759	4,102	—
Public welfare	346,759	162,494	184,265	142,460	40,768	1,037	—	—
Hospitals	980,555	503,356	477,199	237,619	127,461	1,535	110,584	—
Police protection	548,627	69,268	479,359	108,790	344,415	26,154	—	—
Local fire protection	209,767	—	209,767	15,087	179,578	9,019	6,083	—
Sanitation other than sewerage	121,169	—	121,169	10,378	105,288	5,162	341	—
All other functions	2,560,949	926,682	1,634,267	562,602	813,753	51,202	206,123	587
Full-time Employees Who Belong to an Employee Organization, Total	4,709,631	1,008,548	3,701,083	515,893	1,099,045	128,058	114,144	1,843,943
By function:								
Education	2,555,952	234,808	2,321,144	149,614	251,740	75,847	—	1,843,943
Instructional staff	1,959,135	96,586	1,862,549	127,828	201,150	62,683	—	1,470,888
Other	596,817	138,222	458,595	21,786	50,590	13,164	—	373,055
Highways	234,027	131,971	102,056	38,667	50,736	10,586	2,067	—
Public welfare	132,525	61,808	70,717	54,283	16,349	85	—	—
Hospitals	374,274	242,679	131,595	60,567	61,092	466	9,470	—
Police protection	291,852	32,923	258,929	44,387	198,356	16,186	—	—
Local fire protection	152,910	—	152,910	8,089	135,450	6,401	2,970	—
Sanitation other than sewerage	55,572	—	55,572	2,031	49,937	3,480	124	—
All other functions	912,519	304,359	608,160	158,255	335,385	15,007	99,513	—
Percent of Full-time Employees Who Belong to an Employee Organization, Total	47.8	37.7	51.5	34.6	53.1	58.9	34.9	59.9

By function:								
Education	56.2	30.9	61.2	51.8	76.1	79.3	59.9	—
Instructional staff	64.3	33.1	67.6	60.9	79.6	83.3	66.3	—
Other	39.7	29.6	44.3	27.5	64.9	64.6	43.4	—
Highways	43.2	51.6	35.8	30.5	40.0	38.1	—	50.4
Public welfare	38.2	38.0	38.4	38.1	40.1	8.2	—	—
Hospitals	38.2	48.2	27.6	25.5	47.9	30.4	—	8.6
Police protection	53.2	47.5	54.0	40.8	57.6	61.9	—	—
Local fire protection	72.9	—	72.9	53.6	75.4	71.0	—	48.8
Sanitation other than Sewerage	45.9	—	45.9	19.6	47.4	67.4	—	36.4
All other functions	35.6	32.8	37.2	28.1	41.2	29.3	—	48.3
Labor-Management Agreements in Effect, October 1977	30,442	873	29,569	2,431	7,481	3,022	15,308	1,327
Contractual agreements	23,564	683	22,881	1,861	5,585	2,568	11,958	909
Memoranda of understanding	6,878	190	6,688	570	1,896	454	3,350	418
Labor-Management Agreements that Became Effective during Year Ended October 1977	17,062	477	16,585	1,382	3,983	1,544	9,015	661
Contractual agreements, total	13,645	416	13,229	1,085	2,984	1,316	7,387	457
New contractual agreements	2,236	116	2,120	178	381	156	1,336	69
Renegotiated contractual agreements	11,409	300	11,109	907	2,603	1,160	6,051	388
Memoranda of understanding	3,417	61	3,356	297	999	228	1,628	204
Employees Covered by Contractual Agreements:								
By all agreements in effect, October 1977	3,755,280	741,918	3,013,362	324,337	901,052	133,359	1,556,023	98,591
By new agreements that became effective during year ended October 1977	357,478	98,707	258,771	21,516	22,851	4,638	205,474	4,292
By renegotiated agreements that became effective during year ended October 1977	1,721,738	410,375	1,311,355	144,304	287,286	59,161	790,317	30,287
Percent of Employees Covered by Contractual Agreements:								
By all agreements in effect, October 1977	29.4	21.3	32.5	18.4	34.4	37.0	37.7	25.1
By new agreements that became effective during year ended October	2.8	2.8	2.8	1.2	0.9	1.3	5.0	1.1
By renegotiated agreements that became effective during year ended October 1977	13.5	11.8	14.1	8.2	11.0	16.4	19.2	7.5
Bargaining Units, Total	30,131	1,044	29,091	2,592	7,527	2,924	14,862	1,186
By number of employees represented:								
500 or more employees	1,542	262	1,280	217	395	18	611	39
300 to 499 employees	1,196	98	1,098	136	249	55	627	31
100 to 299 employees	5,003	223	4,780	461	963	257	2,985	114
50 to 99 employees	5,183	125	5,058	454	1,138	313	3,006	147
25 to 49 employees	5,897	116	5,781	530	1,486	609	2,958	198
Less than 25 employees	11,310	216	11,094	794	3,296	1,672	4,675	657
Employees Represented by Bargaining Units	4,726,079	865,032	3,861,047	529,882	1,157,294	140,711	1,915,701	117,459
As a Percent of All Employees	37.0	24.8	41.6	30.1	44.1	39.0	46.4	29.2

Table 1-4 *(continued)*

Item	State and Local Governments	State Governments	Local Governments					
			Total	Counties	Municipalities	Townships	Special Districts	School Districts
Work Stoppages during Year Ended October 1977[a]	485	33	452	61	154	20	24	193
By function:								
Education	225	11	214	3	7	11	—	193
Instructional staff	174	3	171	1	5	7	—	158
Other	131	9	122	2	2	4	—	114
Highways	58	2	56	17	35	4	—	—
Public welfare	13	3	10	9	1		—	—
Hospitals	20	10	10	8	2		—	—
Police protection	36	1	35	5	26	4	—	—
Local fire protection	24		24	1	22	1	—	—
Sanitation other than sewerage	55	—	55	5	46	3	1	—
All other functions	154	11	143	27	87	6	23	—
Employees Involved in Work Stoppages during Year Ended October 1977	178,814	35,203	143,611	18,907	26,646	3,163	9,189	85,706
By function:								
Education	98,393	5,568	92,830	214	4,241	2,665	—	85,706
Instructional staff	69,780	551	69,229	30	4,079	2,435	—	62,685
Other	28,614	5,017	23,597	184	162	230	—	23,021
Highways	4,167	1,689	2,478	1,129	1,270	79	—	—
Public welfare	8,607	7,600	1,007	959	48		—	—
Hospitals	9,447	4,423	5,024	4,544	480		—	—
Police protection	2,058	94	1,964	492	1,335	137	—	—
Local fire protection	3,342		3,342	120	3,207	15	—	—
Sanitation other than sewerage	5,494	—	5,494	520	4,866	97	11	—
All other functions	47,305	15,829	31,476	10,929	11,199	170	9,178	—
Duration of Work Stoppages during Year Ended October 1977 (Days)	3,608	136	3,472	557	1,072	95	222	1,526
By function:								
Education	2,436	50	1,629	6	68	85	—	1,526
Instructional staff	1,370	9	1,361	1	53	45	—	1,262
Other	1,066	44	1,022	5	15	40	—	962
Highways	539	2	537	131	384	22	—	—
Public welfare	114	13	101	100	1		—	—
Hospitals	176	21	155	100	55		—	—
Police protection	128	1	127	37	80	10	—	—
Local fire protection	82		82	2	79	1	—	—
Sanitation other than sewerage	357	—	357	102	245	8	2	—
All other functions	1,292	57	1,235	246	745	24	220	—

Days of Idleness for Work Stoppages during
Year Ended October 1977

	1,457,475	183,530	1,273,945	96,527	174,870	16,697	49,887	935,964
By function:								
Education	1,056,300	52,664	1,003,636	522	51,901	15,249	—	935,964
Instructional staff	763,975	1,613	762,362	30	50,686	12,839	—	698,807
Other	292,325	51,051	241,274	492	1,215	2,410	—	237,157
Highways	25,233	1,689	23,544	8,295	14,985	264	—	—
Public welfare	21,599	14,820	6,779	6,731	48	—	—	—
Hospitals	53,553	6,608	46,945	32,507	14,438	—	—	—
Police protection	6,950	94	6,856	3,625	2,922	309	—	—
Local fire protection	7,053	—	7,053	240	6,798	15	—	—
Sanitation other than sewerage	32,365	—	32,365	7,288	24,776	279	22	—
All other functions	254,422	107,655	146,767	37,319	59,002	581	49,865	—

Source: Bureau of National Affairs, *Government Employee Relations Report*, (GERR) *Reference File*—186 (Washington, D.C.: Bureau of National Affairs, 10 December 1979), p. 71:4097-4098. Tables I-4 to I-9, inclusive, were originally published in Department of Commerce, *Bureau of the Census, Public Employment, Labor-Management Relations in State and Local Governments* (Washington, D.C.: Government Printing Office, 1979). Because the GERR is more likely to be accessible, tables and quotations from the original Bureau of the Census report are referenced to the GERR.

[a]Each work stoppage is counted separately at the governmental function affected by the stoppage but is counted only once in the total number of work stoppages (for example, a stoppage involving two selected functions will be counted separately at each of the functions but only once in the total).

Table 1-5
Distribution of States by Percent of Full-Time Employees Organized

| | Number of States by Type of Employees[a] | | | | | |
| | All Employees | | Teachers Only | | All Other Employees | |
Percent of Full-Time Employees Organized	1977	1972	1977	1972	1977	1972
Total	51	51	51	51	51	51
Less than 25	8	2	1	—	29	30
25 to 39.9	17	19	3	—	13	15
40 to 54.9	9	18	12	6	7	5
55 to 69.9	13	8	21	20	1	1
70 to 84.9	4	4	12	22	1	—
85 or more	—	—	2	13	—	—

Source: Bureau of National Affairs, *Government Employee Relations Report, Reference File* —186 (Washington, D.C.: Bureau of National Affairs, 10 December 1979), p. 71:4091.
[a]Includes the District of Columbia.

Two additional tables may help to clarify the tremendous interstate differences related to public-sector bargaining. Table 1-8 shows the number and percent of state and local governments that engaged in some form of discussion with organized employees in 1977. As used by the Bureau of Census and in this analysis, the term

> *meet and confer discussions* . . . refers to the process by which the public employer consents to discuss conditions of employment with representatives of an employee organization. If the parties reach an agreement, it may be written in the form of a memorandum of understanding. The employer is, however, not legally bound to enter into these discussions, nor to abide by any resulting memorandum of understanding.

Table 1-6
Organized Full-Time Employees by Level and Type of Government

| | Organized Full-Time Employees | | | |
| | Number | | Percent | |
Level and Type of Government	1977	1972	1977	1972
Total	4,709,631	4,319,941	47.8	50.4
State governments	1,008,548	942,532	37.7	40.8
Local governments	3,701,083	3,377,409	51.5	53.9
Counties	515,893	458,504	34.6	39.0
Municipalities	1,099,045	1,047,346	53.1	54.5
Townships	128,058	98,570	58.9	51.6
Special districts	114,144	88,776	34.9	33.1
School districts	1,843,943	1,684,213	59.9	62.1

Source: Bureau of National Affairs, *Government Employee Relations Report, Reference File* —186 (Washington, D.C.: Bureau of National Affairs, 10 December 1979), p. 71:4091.

Collective negotiations, on the other hand, refers to negotiations in which both management and employee representatives are equal legal parties in the bargaining process and decisions are reached jointly through bilaterial negotiations. The end result of collective negotiations is a mutually binding contractual agreement. [Italics added.][1]

As evidenced by table 1-8, North Carolina and Virginia emerge as the states least hospitable to any form of bargaining by public-sector employees. Nevertheless, table 1-8 tends to understate the extent of public-sector bargaining because it does not take into account the number of employees in the various local governments; most of the governments that do not bargain employ a small number of employees.

Table 1-9 suggests the continued increase in public-sector bargaining from 1972 to 1977. The number of governments entering into agreements increased from 19,547 in 1972 to 30,442 in 1977; note that the number of memoranda of understanding increased from 6224 to 6878 during this period whereas contractual agreements increased from 13,323 to 23,564 in 1977. These figures reflect the continuing trend toward negotiated contracts instead of memoranda of understanding; in both state governments and school districts, there was a decrease in the number of memoranda of understanding but an increase in the number of contractual agreements.

The number of bargaining units for government varied considerably. As of October 1977 there were 30,131 employee-bargaining units in 36 state governments and 12,110 local governments. These bargaining units represented 4,726,079, or 37 percent, of all state and local government

Table 1-7
Percent of Full-Time Employees Organized by Function and Level of Government

Function	State and Local Governments		State Governments		Local Governments	
	1977	1972	1977	1972	1977	1972
Total	47.8	50.4	37.7	40.8	51.5	53.9
For selected function:						
Education	56.2	56.6	30.9	26.7	61.2	63.1
Teachers	64.2	69.5	33.1	30.9	67.6	73.7
Other	39.6	31.4	29.6	24.3	44.3	35.1
Highways	43.2	46.0	51.6	57.9	35.8	33.5
Public welfare	38.2	45.1	38.0	44.4	38.4	45.5
Hospitals	38.2	41.7	48.2	52.2	27.6	30.7
Police protection	53.2	55.6	47.5	54.2	54.0	55.8
Local fire protection	72.9	76.5	—	—	72.9	76.5
Sanitation other than sewerage	45.9	50.1	—	—	45.9	50.1
All other functions	35.6	39.4	32.8	39.7	37.2	39.2

Source: Bureau of National Affairs, *Government Employee Relations Report, Reference File* —186 (Washington, D.C.: Bureau of National Affairs, 10 December 1979), p. 71:4092.

Table 1-8

Number and Percent of State and Local Governments that Engaged in Collective Negotiations and/or Meet-and-Confer Discussions, by State, October 1977

| | All State and Local Governments | | | State and Local Governments Excluding Special Districts | | |
| | | Governments that Engaged in CN and/or MC Discussions | | | Governments that Engaged in CN and/or MC Discussions | |
States	Total	Number	Percent	Total	Number	Percent
United States, total	79,928	13,094	16.4	53,918	12,331	22.9
Alabama	953	37	3.9	614	34	5.5
Alaska	151	30	19.9	151	30	19.9
Arizona	420	102	24.3	314	101	32.2
Arkansas	1,347	57	4.2	923	57	6.2
California	3,807	1,384	36.4	1,578	1,169	74.1
Colorado	1,465	116	7.9	510	109	21.4
Connecticut	435	169	38.9	199	153	76.9
Delaware	211	31	14.7	84	30	35.7
District of Columbia	2	2	100.0	1	1	100.0
Florida	912	186	20.4	551	176	31.9
Georgia	1,267	21	1.7	877	14	1.6
Hawaii	20	4	20.0	5	4	80.0
Idaho	973	110	11.3	361	104	28.8
Illinois	6,619	795	12.0	3,872	763	19.7
Indiana	2,867	325	11.3	1,977	312	15.8
Iowa	1,851	443	23.9	1,517	442	29.1
Kansas	3,726	276	7.4	2,507	273	10.9
Kentucky	1,185	48	4.1	707	45	6.4
Louisiana	459	26	5.7	429	25	5.8
Maine	782	174	22.3	604	166	27.5
Maryland	427	37	8.7	175	33	18.9
Massachusetts	768	370	48.2	440	350	79.5
Michigan	2,627	843	32.1	2,460	830	33.7
Minnesota	3,439	572	16.6	3,176	560	17.6
Mississippi	836	15	1.8	532	15	2.8
Missouri	2,938	237	8.1	1,927	223	11.6
Montana	950	205	21.6	639	200	31.3
Nebraska	3,425	346	10.1	2,232	336	15.1
Nevada	183	36	19.7	51	30	58.8
New Hampshire	507	100	19.7	404	99	24.5
New Jersey	1,516	781	51.5	1,136	742	65.3
New Mexico	315	39	12.4	215	39	18.1
New York	3,307	1,051	31.8	2,342	1,038	44.3
North Carolina	875	—	—	573	—	—
North Dakota	2,706	159	5.9	2,119	159	7.5
Ohio	3,333	686	20.6	3,018	661	21.9
Oklahoma	1,695	160	9.4	1,290	160	12.4
Oregon	1,449	374	25.8	652	336	51.5
Pennsylvania	5,239	1,086	20.7	3,200	970	30.3
Rhode Island	120	44	36.7	43	37	86.1
South Carolina	585	11	1.9	403	9	2.2
South Dakota	1,729	180	10.4	1,581	178	11.3
Tennessee	907	35	3.9	436	31	7.1

Table 1-8 *(continued)*

States	All State and Local Governments			State and Local Governments Excluding Special Districts		
		Governments that Engaged in CN and/or MC Discussions			Governments that Engaged in CN and/or MC Discussions	
	Total	*Number*	*Percent*	*Total*	*Number*	*Percent*
Texas	3,897	145	3.7	2,455	140	5.7
Utah	493	42	8.5	287	39	13.6
Vermont	648	143	22.1	581	143	24.6
Virginia	390	—	—	325	—	—
Washington	1,669	430	25.8	607	342	56.3
West Virginia	597	27	4.5	338	23	6.8
Wisconsin	2,519	553	22.0	2,329	549	23.6
Wyoming	387	50	12.9	171	50	29.2

Source: Bureau of National Affairs, *Government Employee Relations Report, Reference File —186* (Washington, D.C.: Bureau of National Affairs, 10 December 1979), p. 71:4093.

employees. As might be expected, state governments tended to have more bargaining units per government. Whereas only 205 of 12,110 local governments had 10 or more bargaining units, 28 of the 36 state governments had this many. Most of the 12,110 local governments had only one bargaining unit, whereas only 2 of 36 state governments had only 1-2 bargaining units.[2]

Although comprehensive data are not available, union revenues have been increasing at a faster rate than union membership. One reason is the increasing number of agency shop clauses, that is, clauses which require nonmembers to pay service fees to the unions. Another reason is that the amounts paid per employee have also been increasing. Thus in 1976-1977, 36 of the NEA's state affiliates had pegged state dues as a percentage of a moving average such as the average teacher salary in the state. Other unions were also moving to this type of dues structure, to avoid the need for the leadership to secure authorization from the membership (or appropriate union legislative body) for more revenues.

The total revenues of public-sector unions are not available, but $750 million annually is probably a low figure. The 1979-1980 budget for the NEA, not including its state and local affiliates, was $62.7 million. State association dues vary widely, but if an estimated 1,750,000 NEA members pay an average of $100 a year in state association dues, the total would reach almost $238 million without including any local association dues, AFT dues at the national, state, or local level, or the dues paid by any other local, state, or national public-sector union including AFSCME, which is the largest. Nor would it include, except for NEA, any union income from interest, advertising in union publications, or union income from other sources such as federal and foundation grants. Clearly, the public-sector unions are big business.

Table 1-9
Labor-Management Agreements by Level and Type of Government

Level and Type of Government	Total				Contractual Agreements				Memoranda of Understanding			
	Number		Percent		Number		Percent		Number		Percent	
	1977	1972	1977	1972	1977	1972	1977	1972	1977	1972	1977	1972
Total	30,442	19,547	100.0	100.0	23,564	13,323	100.0	100.0	6,878	6,224	100.0	100.0
State governments	873	1,006	2.9	5.1	683	616	2.9	4.6	190	390	2.8	6.3
Local governments	29,569	18,541	97.1	94.9	22,881	12,707	97.1	95.4	6,688	5,834	97.2	93.7
Counties	2,431	1,233	8.0	6.3	1,861	858	7.9	6.4	570	375	8.3	6.0
Municipalities	7,481	4,487	24.6	23.0	5,585	3,200	23.7	24.0	1,896	1,287	27.6	20.7
Townships	3,022	1,696	9.9	8.7	2,568	1,452	10.9	10.9	454	244	6.6	3.9
Special districts	1,327	797	4.4	4.1	909	404	3.9	3.0	418	393	6.1	6.3
School districts	15,308	10,328	50.3	52.8	11,958	6,793	50.7	51.0	3,350	3,535	48.7	56.8

Source: Bureau of National Affairs, *Government Employee Relations Report, Reference File—186* (Washington, D.C.: Bureau of National Affairs, 10 December 1979), p. 71:4094.

Causal Factors in Public-Sector Bargaining

Over the years several observers have tried to explain the increase in public-sector bargaining. Whatever their validity in the past, these explanations require some revision in light of recent developments. Thus in 1966, Lieberman and Moskow listed the following causal factors in the emergence of collective bargaining in public education:

1. The need for effective teacher representation at the local level.
2. Changes in teacher attitudes (from indifferent or antibargaining to pro-bargaining).
3. Organization rivalry (which was deemed the most important single factor in the rapid spread of collective bargaining in public education).
4. Consolidation of school districts, increasing the need for collective representation.
5. The snowball effect, that is, the more bargaining, the more difficult for the nonbargainers to stick to their position. This principle applies to state legislation as well as to local school districts.
6. Developments outside education. Here reference was made to the fact that collective bargaining in other areas of public employment was conducive to its acceptance in education. Of course, the reverse was true, and is still today.[3]

Looking at this list today and thinking in terms of public employment generally, most of the factors are still operative, but some revision would be appropriate. Union rivalry is certainly a crucial factor. The reason behind the competition is that it is extremely difficult for one union to replace another as exclusive representative. Therefore, when a bargaining law is enacted, unions move quickly to become the bargaining agent in as many jurisdictions as possible. The rush to become recognized as a bargaining agent is followed by intensive bargaining. Such bargaining is intended to ward off possible challenges from rival unions and to achieve contracts that can be used elsewhere to persuade potential members of the effectiveness of the union.

The rapid spread of bargaining after enactment of a state bargaining law is not due to widespread rank-and-file demands for immediate bargaining. Instead, it is the result of union leadership efforts to achieve incumbency before being frozen out by a rival union. Needless to say, these efforts force unions to develop pro-bargaining attitudes among public employees more quickly than would otherwise be the case. Such attitude changes are both cause and result of the snowball effect alluded to previously.

Probably the most important causal factors to be added are inflation and taxpayer resistance, both of which tend to generate support for bargaining and public-sector strikes. Regardless, the essential point is that unions are in the organizing business. Like any other business, they seek to expand. Paradoxically, unions must sometimes expand into nonunion areas in order to maintain the status quo. In this respect, the union is unlike most businesses. To the Ford dealers, citizens who drive Chevrolets are an opportunity. To the union, the unorganized are a threat as well as an opportunity. Nonunion employers and nonunion employees are perceived as a threat for two reasons. First, such employees allegedly are apt to work for less, thus making it more difficult to achieve benefits for union members. Second, the existence of the unorganized is harmful to union solidarity and discipline. And if the nonunion employees might be organized by a rival union, their nonunion status is even more of a threat.

At this point, we should note that union membership revenues can increase substantially even though there is no increase in public-sector bargaining. Union membership has increased when the negotiated contracts require employers to fire employees who do not pay dues or a service fee to the union. The extent to which such clauses are responsible for increases in union membership varies widely, but they probably account for 5 to 15 percent of total union membership in the public sector. On the other hand, agency shop clauses do not constitute an increase in public-sector bargaining. Of course, the income generated by such clauses may contribute to union-organizing campaigns elsewhere.

Thus far, little has been said about the state laws that require public employers to bargain with unions under certain conditions. Such legislation is both cause and result of the tremendous expansion of public-sector bargaining. Obviously, the legislation would not have been enacted without some of the causal conditions previously mentioned. In that sense, the legislation is a result, not a cause. Nonetheless, once enacted, state bargaining laws are usually the single most important causal factor in the growth of public-sector bargaining within a state.

All the causal factors just discussed tend to interact with and reinforce the others. This is particularly true of the relationship between bargaining legislation and political action. Unquestionably, public-sector unions have increased their political influence considerably in the last twenty years. This is rather ironic since public-sector bargaining was justified partly on the grounds that legislative remedies were too slow and ineffective to resolve labor-management problems in the public service. In the takeoff years (the 1960s), there was some thought that once the legislatures had provided bargaining rights at the local level, they would get out of the business of legislating statewide terms and conditions of employment. They could legitimately say that they had established a mechanism for dealing with these problems at the local level and that they did not intend to usurp the functions of local public employers. In fact, no such legislative reaction seems to have occurred, at least on a national basis.

The Political Influence of Public-Sector Unions

Reference was made earlier to the increased political influence of public-sector unions. In some respects, this is the most important outcome of public-sector bargaining. The increased political influence of public-sector unions is manifest at all levels of government and in virtually every state. It is especially evident in the larger cities, partly because such cities tend to include a relatively high proportion of public employees. For example, New York City employed almost 400,000 persons in 1971. Together with their families, these employees constituted a potential voting bloc of more than 1.2 million, a formidable number, even by New York City standards. Nevertheless, as Spero and Capozzola point out, the numbers of municipal public employees are not as significant as the fact that they are increasingly well organized for political action.[4]

Consider the following excerpt from the *New York Teacher*, a publication of the New York State United Teachers (by far the largest state affiliate of the American Federation of Teachers):

Days before the Primary Election in New York State, the Louis Harris public opinion organization issued the results of its poll in New York State, showing that President Carter led Senator Kennedy by a whopping margin of 61 percent to 34 percent.

However, on Sunday, March 16, the 2,000 delegates to the United Teachers Representative Assembly overwhelmingly voted for the endorsement of Senator Kennedy in his race for the Democratic nommination for the Presidency.

From that moment, the New York State United Teachers committed the strength of its 225,000 members across the State to work day and night in behalf of Senator Kennedy.

As *The New York Times* commented relative to the rival camps' efforts, the day after Senator Kennedy's stunning upset victory:

"The major effort was mounted by the New York State United Teachers, which swung into action after endorsing Mr. Kennedy last weekend."

Immediately after he had banged the last gavel of the 1980 RA, NYSUT President Thomas Y. Hobart and Executive Director Vito DeLeonardis, together with Ray Skuse, director of legislation, called together all of the United Teachers Regional Coordinators and established the mechanism for the statewide telephone bank campaign in behalf of Kennedy.

Telephone banks were established in every one of the 15 NYSUT Regional Service Centers throughout the state, as well as in all five UFT borough offices in New York City. The need to support Kennedy was quickly recognized by the members as volunteers spent countless hours on the telephones urging NYSUT members and their families to vote for Kennedy on Primary Day, March 25.

In NYSUT Regional Service Centers and Albany headquarters, there were 203 telephones in use every afternoon after school, at nights and over the last weekend before Primary Day.

In New York City, under the direction of Staff Director Sandra Feldman, the UFT installed and opened up 179 telephones in its five borough offices for the Kennedy volunteers, who called upon UFT's 65,000 members and their families to turn out and vote for Kennedy.

We were sending a message, were the comments of many volunteers. It was a message not only of support for Senator Kennedy in his fight, but also a message to Washington and the Carter Administration not to write off the public schools, not to write off the second-most populous state, and not to write off the urban centers of our nation.

In addition to the state union's telephone banks, a special edition of the *New York Teacher* was written, designed, printed and mailed within 48 hours of the endorsement of Senator Kennedy by NYSUT's Representative Assembly. The special issue, dated March 18, conveyed the concerns that had been the concerns of delegates when they voted the state union's endorsement of Senator Kennedy for the Democratic Primary.

Kennedy overcame that seemingly crushing 61 to 34 percent deficit with the help of NYSUT's 225,000 members in eight short days, to emerge as the state-wide victor by a 59 to 41 percent margin.

The NYSUT-Kennedy margin of victory broke down as follows:

In New York City, Kennedy—63 percent, Carter—37 percent.

In Nassau, Suffolk and Westchester, Kennedy—63 percent, Carter—37 percent.

Upstate, Kennedy—48 Percent, Carter—52 percent, and that by a Carter Margin of less than 16,000 votes out of more than 235,000 votes cast.

In New York City, Kennedy swept all 17 Congressional Districts.

On Long Island, Kennedy swept all six Congressional Districts.

In the northern suburbs of Westchester, Putnam, Dutchess and Orange Counties, Kennedy swept all three Congressional Districts.

In the upstate Congressional Districts, Kennedy took C.D. 27 (Catskills, Binghamton and Ithaca), C.D. 29 (Troy and Saratoga) and C.D. 36 (Niagara Falls).[5]

Even making allowances for the natural tendency to inflate its own influence, the NYSUT effort is impressive. Certainly, politicians are becoming much more responsive to public-sector unions, a fact that is significant in many ways in this analysis.[6]

One additional comment about NYSUT support for Senator Kennedy is in order; it illustrates a fact of enormous importance about the role of union leadership in the political arena. The NEA endorsed President Carter in the New York Democratic primary, as it did in the other state primaries and in the 1980 general election. Thus the two national teacher organizations considered the same candidates and the same records; presumably acting in the best interests of similar constituencies, they nevertheless supported rival candidates. How can this be? If President Carter were as good for teachers as NEA asserts, how could NYSUT and the AFT endorse Kennedy, and do so overwhelmingly? The question is even more intriguing in view of the fact that the AFT endorsed President Carter after the Democratic convention in August 1980. And if Senator Kennedy were so clearly the better choice for teachers, as asserted by the AFT, how could the NEA overwhelmingly endorse and support President Carter?

Again, it must be emphasized that the conflicting endorsements cannot be viewed as merely an honest rank-and-file difference of opinion. If there were a substantial minority in NEA that supported Senator Kennedy and a substantial minority in the AFT that supported President Carter, the conflicting outcomes might be explained as a good-faith difference, with demographic or ethnic or other organizational variations explaining the different endorsements. The overwhelming nature of the endorsements, plus the fact that each union includes a substantial membership similar in all important respects to a substantial bloc in the rival union, precludes any such explanation. What does seem clear is this: Within very broad limits, union leadership has enormous capability of generating support for objectives set by the leadership. This conclusion is not unique to public-sector unions, but it is an extremely important dimension to bargaining as well as to their political role.[7]

The ability of union leaders to devote union resources to objectives not shared by the membership is not due to the fact that union governance structures are undemocratic. The problem lies elsewhere. The larger and more geographically dispersed a union is, the more difficult it is for individual union members to affect the course of union affairs. The overwhelming majority of members do not have the time or resources to launch a campaign against the incumbent leadership. Thus the tendency, especially as unions become larger, is toward nonparticipation. Membership apathy is widely deplored (albeit sometimes with crocodile tears), but it has an existential basis that is difficult to overcome. Even when union leadership has negotiated poor contracts, potential opposition to union leadership usually stands to lose more personally from the effort to oust the leadership or change its policies than it stands to gain, even if successful. Paradoxically, an effort to oust incumbent leadership makes more sense if its underlying objective is something other than improving member welfare through bargaining, even though the latter is almost invariably the avowed reason for efforts to change union leadership.

Both union supporters and critics tend to obscure the realities of leadership-membership relations in unions. As Olson has pointed out, we cannot automatically assume that members of a group or organization will take action that is in the best interests of the group.[8] In this respect, relationships between unions and union members are not essentially different from the relationships between organizations and their members in other fields or between citizens and governments. The individual who acts on behalf of the rank and file gets only the same benefits that go to everyone. Although the union member may believe that union leadership could achieve more for members, the time and expense required to oust incumbent leadership or to influence its actions is often greater than the potential benefit to the individual dissident. Note that the same problem exists with even greater force for members discontent with the political tilt of union leadership; the benefits of opposition to union leadership over this issue are even more speculative.

Doing nothing about objectionable union actions may be a rational course of action for members. This may be regrettable, but it does not present a problem unique to unions. An endless number of editorialists decry the fact that barely half the eligible population votes in presidential elections, yet virtually none consider the possibility that this may be a rational course of action for large numbers of people. Actually, union leadership sometimes is able to play a constructive role only *because* of its ability to disregard rank-and-file opposition or indifference. Of course, I do not suggest that union leadership would visibly pursue a course of action diametrically opposed to rank and file wishes on a sensitive issue. Leadership activism usually cannot go beyond membership indifference or membership opposition that is not deep. This is not to suggest that unions have an undemocratic governance structure. To emphasize the democratic nature of unions, union leaders frequently point out that they can be voted out of office and that the members can even vote to decertify the union, that is, to eliminate its status as exclusive representative. Arguably, unions are subject to more safeguards in this respect than most organizations or perhaps even most governments. The point is not that unions have an undemocratic governance structure but that we should not assume membership approval of union leaders or activities merely from the existence of a democratic governance structure or from the absence of overt opposition to such leaders or activities.

Notes

1. Bureau of National Affairs, *Government Employee Relations Report, Reference File*-186 (Washington, D.C.: Bureau of National Affairs, 10 December 1979), p. 71:4092.

2. Ibid., p. 71:4094.

3. Myron Lieberman and Michael H. Moskow, *Collective Negotiations for Teachers* (Chicago: Rand McNally, 1966), pp. 55-61.

4. Sterling Spero and John M. Capozzola, *The Urban Community and Its Unionized Bureaucracies* (New York: Dunellen Publishing, 1978), p. 74.

5. "Confounding the Pollsters," *New York Teacher*, 30 March 1980, p. 3. As originally drafted, this discussion included a quotation from the *NEA Reporter* 19, no. 2 (March 1980). On June 23, 1980, the NEA denied permission to quote an excerpt from page 2, which described the NEA's all-out support for President Carter and its increasing political influence generally. Although this was the first and only such incident I have experienced in the 25 years that I have published books and journal articles, no reason was given for the denial.

6. For a more extended discussion of this development, see Spero and Capozzola, *The Urban Community*, pp. 75-105; and Alan Edward Bent and T. Zane Reeves, *Collective Bargaining in the Public Sector* (Menlo Park, Calif.: Benjamin/Cummings Publishing, 1978), especially pp. 141-206, 262-307. See also Myron Lieberman, "The Union Merger Movement: Will 3,500,000 Teachers Put It All Together?" *Saturday Review* 55 (June 24, 1972):50-56; and the address by Florida Governor D. Robert Graham to the 1980 NEA Convention, Los Angeles, July 6, 1980.

7. For an interesting discussion of how the interests of union leaders and union members may conflict and why union leadership is often able to pursue policies that conflict with the interests of the members, see John Burton, "Discussion Paper in Political Economy 6, Some Further Reflecting on Syndicalism," *Government Union Review,* no. 2 (Spring 1980):42-55.

8. Mancur Olson, Jr., *The Logic of Collective Action* (Cambridge, Mass.: Harvard University Press, 1965).

2

The Early Debate
over Public-Sector
Bargaining

The 1960s were the takeoff period for public-sector bargaining. In 1960 no state had enacted bargaining rights for state or local government employees; public-sector bargaining was a special arrangement, tolerated by a small number of local governments. Strikes were rare, with the vast majority of public-sector unions accepting their illegality and/or officially rejecting their use as pressure tactics.

By 1970 matters were very different indeed. Thirty-eight states had enacted some type of bargaining or meet-and-confer legislation. Membership in public-sector unions had virtually quadrupled; whereas there were only 36 strikes by public employees in 1960, there were 412 in 1970, and they tended to last longer and involve more employees than strikes prior to the 1960s. Without reciting an avalanche of data, we can say that by 1970, public-sector bargaining had emerged as a major development in public policy, public administration, and in the labor movement generally.

Understandably, the rise of public-sector bargaining was characterized by widespread controversy. Unfortunately, many supporters and opponents alike did not know very much about collective bargaining, except perhaps that they were for or against it. The uncertainties in its possible introduction into the public sector further compounded the general confusion. It was always possible for bargaining supporters to argue that changes from the National Labor Relations Act (NLRA) could be drafted to meet specific objections to public-sector bargaining. For instance, where a legislature insisted on a prohibition of strikes, such a prohibition of strikes was added to proposed legislation.

Realistically, public-sector bargaining laws are enacted at the initiative of public-sector unions. Over the years the union rationale has emphasized a few major themes that will be discussed throughout this book. First, however, we should note the distinction between the causal factors and the rationale for public-sector bargaining.

To some extent these two dimensions overlap. If people act on the basis of a persuasive rationale, the latter is a causal factor in the action taken. Nevertheless, the dimensions are different. The causal factors may be regarded as those conditions that generated an interest in, or a willingness to consider, public-sector bargaining. For instance, inadequate representation at the local level was listed as a causal factor. Such inadequacy, even where it clearly exists, does not automatically justify public-sector bargaining.

Other alternatives might remedy the problem more effectively. The rationale was used to persuade public employees and legislatures that bargaining and not some other alternative was the solution to the problem. Similarly, inflation is a causal factor because it encourages public employees to look for more effective ways to meet their economic needs. A rationale is still needed to persuade employees that bargaining is the best way to solve this problem.

What then was the rationale for public-sector bargaining in its takeoff period? The following arguments were typically made to justify public-sector bargaining:

1. Public employees face unique disadvantages in their efforts to obtain fair working conditions. Their employers are taxpayers who far outnumber, and hence can always outvote, public employees on wages and related matters. Bargaining is an appropriate way to remedy this unique disadvantage of public employees.
2. Employees' interests in public personnel policies are much greater than the average citizen's. Bargaining is an appropriate way to recognize the fact that public employees are more directly affected than any other group by public personnel policies.
3. Equity requires that public employees have the same rights as private-sector ones. Private-sector employees have bargaining rights. Not to provide the same rights to public employees is to treat them inequitably.
4. Public-employee unions frequently have much to contribute to the operations of a public agency. Bargaining ensures that public employees will have an opportunity to make these contributions.
5. Democratic personnel administration requires that those affected by a policy have an opportunity to express their views about it, prior to its enactment. Bargaining ensures that this will be done.
6. In our society group bargaining power has replaced individual bargaining power as the determinant of who gets what. Bargaining is thus a means to equality since it helps ensure that public employees will not be too weak to protect their interests.
7. The use of arbitrators, mediators, and fact-finders is a valuable technique for resolving labor-management disputes in the private sector. There is no reason to think it would not be just as helpful in the public sector.
8. Bargaining will increase the public interest in matters affecting public services.

It is not my intention here to provide a systematic analysis of the arguments for public-sector bargaining. This has already been done adequately elsewhere.[1] My purpose here is to analyze some of the major issues in the early debate over public-sector bargaining. Subsequently, we shall consider some issues that were not raised until the mid-1970s. By implication, if not directly, the analysis will deal with most if not all the arguments listed previously.

The opponents of public-sector bargaining usually found themselves at a tactical disadvantage when bargaining laws were introduced. Most governmental agencies and legislators had little or no first-hand experience with collective bargaining. Typically they did not have the vaguest idea of the implications of certain provisions in the legislation. Frequently public bodies or organizations representing public management turned for advice to consultants who were in a position to profit enormously from the enactment of such legislation.

In general, the opponents of public-sector bargaining made the following arguments:

1. Government is sovereign. It is inappropriate for a sovereign power to limit itself by bargaining with one interest group.
2. Government provides essential services. Bargaining will lead to strikes; hence it will foster disruptions of essential services. Such disruptions would be intolerable.
3. Government services are essential to public health and safety. No interruption of such service is acceptable.
4. Most government services are monopolies. Citizens have no alternative supplier of these services in case they are disrupted. This fact gives public employees too much leverage in bargaining or in striking if it comes to that.

Before discussing these arguments in some detail, it should be noted that labor-relations experts are divided over whether there can be true collective bargaining without the right to strike in some form. Some experts believe that without the right to strike, unions have so little bargaining power that employers will not bargain in good faith. Others take the view that the bargaining power between employers and unions is rarely equal to begin with; the absence of a right to strike affects the willingness of the parties to accept or reject contract proposals, but it does not change their good-faith desire to reach agreement. In their view (which is shared by this author), it is possible to have bona fide collective bargaining even in the absence of a legal right to strike. The outcome of the bargaining might be very different because there is no legal right to strike, but the process would still be collective bargaining as the phrase is commonly defined.

It would be difficult to overestimate the importance of this issue. Many of the arguments against public-sector bargaining are based on objections to the use of strikes in the public sector. If these objections are irrelevant, because it is possible to have collective bargaining even in the absence of a right to strike, it becomes much easier to accept the feasibility of public-sector bargaining. On the other hand, those who believe that collective bargaining includes the right to strike must show that public-sector strikes in some form are acceptable, a much heavier burden of proof and of persuasion.

It is surprising how often this issue is ignored, even by analysts who should know better. Frequently their discussion of public-sector bargaining is largely a discussion of the inevitability, or the pros and cons, of public-sector strikes. Indeed, it appears that some analysts simply assume without argument or discussion that the desirability of public-sector bargaining is essentially a matter of the acceptability of strikes by public employees.

A little reflection suggests, however, that the issue of whether there should be public-sector bargaining can and should be distinguished from the issue of whether to legalize strikes by public employees. About 33 states with bargaining laws prohibit strikes by public employees. It is erroneous and pointless to contend that there is no bargaining in these states, except insofar as the public-sector unions violate the law by striking. To assert that the activities in these states are not real collective bargaining is to confuse a definitional problem with a policy one. Collective bargaining can be defined so that it includes the right to strike. However, the underlying issue is not how to define collective bargaining but to what extent, if any, should public employees have the right to strike.

A third view must also be noted. This view accepts the logical distinction between the right to bargain and the right to strike, that is, it concedes that public employees could meaningfully have the former without the latter. On the other hand, it also assumes that the states are unlikely to enact bargaining laws that provide for meaningful bargaining but no right to strike. Adherents of this view believe that it is not impossible to do so but that the states are unlikely to adopt the specific policies that would achieve these objectives. They will either legalize strikes under certain conditions or declare them illegal in ways that do not effectively eliminate or minimize them. Adherents of this view emphasize the fact that even if strikes are illegal, there will be strikes because of employer provocations, misjudgments or inexperience of union leaders, and other factors inherent in the bargaining process.

Analytically, it would have been desirable to separate the issues throughout; for example, by first discussing the desirability of public-sector bargaining and then considering the pros and cons of legalizing strikes by public employees. Editorially, this was not feasible for several reasons. First, it is possible that the desirability of public-sector bargaining from a public-policy point of view may depend on the specific form of implementation; for example, some individuals might support public-sector bargaining but not if it included a legalization of strikes or was otherwise significantly conducive to them. For this reason, the following discussion sometimes includes an analysis of strike issues in considering certain aspects of public-sector bargaining generally. Regardless, the logical possibility that public-sector bargaining without the right to strike may be desirable public policy must be considered on its merits. Needless to say, this possibility assumes that it is possible to eliminate or minimize strikes in a public-sector-bargaining law, even if the state bargaining laws have not been successful to date in this regard. Actually, some of them have been, although bargainists may contend that they have not done so long enough to demonstrate their effectiveness.

The proponents of bargaining differed among themselves as well as with the opponents of bargaining on the strike issue, as they did on most others related to public-sector bargaining. Proponents typically contended that bargaining laws would reduce strikes in the public sector. It was pointed out that in the absence of a bargaining law, public employers could—and sometimes did—pretend that a public-sector union did not represent a majority of employees in an otherwise appropriate bargaining unit. Although disputes over wages and working conditions were and are the leading cause of strikes by public employees, union recognition and bargaining procedures were also a significant cause.[2] Inasmuch as bargaining statutes provide an expeditious way of determining the extent of employee support for a union and eliminate unilateral employer determination of bargaining procedures, they could be expected to reduce the incidence of strikes over these issues, as in fact has been the case.

Another frequent argument was that strikes would be reduced because public employers would have to negotiate in good faith, which they were not previously required to do. In other words, bargaining allegedly would provide an effective mechanism for expressing employee views and concerns. With this mechanism in place, strikes would not be necessary. These arguments did not induce bargainists to abandon their support for the right to strike. On this issue, they argued as follows: "We have to have the right to strike in order not to have to use it. If public employers know that we cannot strike, they will act arbitrarily and arrogantly and without really listening to their employees. Such behavior is what leads to strikes, regardless of whether they are legal or not. On the other hand, if public employees have the right to strike, public employers will not act this way; hence there will not be any need to exercise the right."

Actually, this rationale continues to be the explicit basis for some recommendations to legalize strikes by public employees. For instance, one prestigious legislative-advisory group asserted:

> Our preference for agreed-upon settlements has led us to conclude that all state and local employees should have the right to strike, subject to the limitations discussed below. A credible strike possibility provides maximum

motivational force for the parties in collective bargaining to attempt in good faith to reach agreement. Collective bargaining seems most likely to work if both parties are uncertain about what will happen if they do not reach agreement.

A no-strike system places this apprehension exclusively on the employees. These anxieties are not present on the employer's side of the table. When a lawful strike is a credible possibility, however, the anxieties are shared by both the employees and their employer, with the result that both parties are more likely to reach toward mutually acceptable compromises.

We have not been persuaded by the evidence submitted to us, or otherwise available, that an adequate substitute for the strike in terms of motivational force has been discovered. This is not to say that collective bargaining in the public sector never works unless strikes are permissible. The Chairman of New York's Board has stated in 1971 that in the nearly four years of operation of the New York law, which prohibits strikes, there had been about 6,300 settlements and 62 strikes, something less than one percent. Considering that in 1970, 15 percent of the settlements in the private sector were reached after strike action, it can be argued that, both in absolute and comparative terms, the record in New York is impressive.

However, these data do not necessarily prove the point. Although there may have been only 62 strikes, it is not clear how many settlements were reached under the pressure of credible strike threats (it is axiomatic that the threat to strike has more motivational force than the actual strike). Furthermore, we do not know how many of the 6,300 settlements were the result of capitulation by weak employee organizations.[3]

A skeptic may wonder. Only seven years previously, another equally distinguished panel of experts on collective bargaining in New York had unanimously recommended that public-sector strikes be prohibited as an "alien force" in our political process.[4] It does not appear that any of these experts had changed their minds by 1973, despite the fact that they were undoubtedly aware of the New York experience discussed by California's Assembly Advisory Council. Read together, these conflicting recommendations suggest that what these government agencies bought was not so much expertise or objectivity as a point of view. In any event, as we shall see later, the advisory groups in both New York and California, as well as in other states, ignored some of the most fundamental issues relating to the desirability of public-sector bargaining and the legalization of public-sector strikes.

Directly or indirectly, concern over strikes was evident in the opposition to public-sector bargaining. Thus the sovereignty argument was based in part on the idea that government must be in a position to resolve any dispute (including disputes against government itself) that threatens the safety or stability of society. Otherwise, so it was argued, private individuals and organizations would constantly be asserting rights superior to government; the end result would be anarchy.

Whatever element of validity the argument had, it never really took hold. In the first place, the argument tended to equate all public-sector-labor disputes as a challenge to public authority. Technically, they may be; practically and politically, however, the argument seemed like massive overkill, at least in certain situations. The idea that leaf rakers in a public park or custodians in public buildings were engaged in a rebellion or threat to public security was not persuasive politically. Furthermore, bargaining supporters argued that sovereignty was merely a subterfuge to justify the rights of public employers to act irresponsibly, without providing reasonable consideration to the views of employees.

For these and other reasons, the sovereignty argument against public-sector bargaining never really took hold. To say the least, the terminology was not favorable to the opponents of bargaining. Legislators tended to view the appeal to sovereignty as akin to a divine-right type of argument. At a time when governmental immunity from tort actions, based on the same philosophy, was declining, it is not surprising that the sovereignty argument did not prevail. Some courts neatly disposed of the argument by declaring that acceptance of public-sector bargaining was an exercise of sovereign rights, not a denial of them. In the last analysis, the sovereignty argument was more ignored than rebutted, but the end result was the same.[5]

For the most part, the opponents of bargaining emphasized the idea that public-sector bargaining would lead to strikes and that strikes in the public sector should not be tolerated. Those who felt this way probably reflected public opinion, but they were in an unenviable position politically. First, they were opposing a high-priority objective of an influential interest group on the basis of consequences that appeared to be speculative. Furthermore, the personnel policies of many states and local governments left a great deal to be desired. Bargaining might not have been the answer to the horror stories cited by the bargainists, but the opponents of bargaining were usually in the position of defending a status quo that inevitably revealed some vulnerabilities.

The antibargaining argument also asserted that public services were essential. Sometimes, the word *essential* was used without qualifications, and sometimes it meant health-and-safety services such as police and firefighters. The concern for public health and safety clearly had some merit, but it was obviously inapplicable to public employment generally. Although some public employees perform services essential to public health and safety, many do not. Most citizens believe that libraries and parks should be tax supported, but these services are hardly essential to public health and safety. Furthermore, many public services such as transportation, recreation, and education can be, and sometimes are, conducted or dispensed by the private sector.

Even the fact that a service is essential does not necessarily mean that it must be continuous. Tax collectors and record keepers are probably essential, but it would not be a calamity if they ceased their operations for a few days. In fact, taxpayers might even cheer such a development. In public education, it was argued that the education of children must not be interrupted by teacher strikes; to do so was to interrupt an essential service. Looking at summer, Christmas, Easter, and Thanksgiving vacations (for example), it is easy to see why the argument was a rather unconvincing one. Perhaps the most telling point made by bargaining supporters was that even the federal government does not have the authority to end a strike that jeopardizes national health or safety. The government can delay such a strike for 80 days, but it cannot enjoin the strike permanently.

In broad perspective, it is possible to distinguish three major positions related to the essential-service argument.

1. Public-sector bargaining and strikes by public employees should be prohibited regardless of whether all government services are essential. In general, proponents of this position regard the impact of bargaining and strikes on our political processes as the crucial consideration in assessing the desirability of public-sector bargaining and the legalization of strikes by public employees.
2. Public-sector bargaining and strikes by public employees should be permitted for all public employees. Proponents of this view usually believe that it is impractical and futile politically to provide bargaining and strike rights to some but not all public employees.
3. All public employees should be permitted to bargain, but there should be limitations on the right to strike by certain categories such as police, firefighters, and prison guards. This is probably the most widely accepted view in the academic community, and there is a considerable body of professional literature in support of this position.[6]

Because the purpose of this study is to articulate some positions on public-sector bargaining that concede that (1) some government services are not essential and (2) public-sector bargaining per se does not *necessarily* result in an unacceptable level of strikes by public employees, no effort will be made to analyze in detail the efforts to categorize public services as essential or nonessential, or as strike eligible or noneligible. It must be emphasized, however, that there are immense practical difficulties in distinguishing essential from nonessential services. Furthermore, although it is theoretically possible to have public-sector bargaining without an unacceptable level of strikes by public employees, the likelihood of such an outcome in many states is not very promising.

Professionalism and Public-Sector Strikes

In public education, which includes almost half of all state and local employees, the strike issue was viewed and debated largely in terms of professionalism. Those opposed to legalizing teacher strikes emphasized that teachers are professionals. Professional employees do not bargain collectively or strike and most certainly not against children or communities. Hence teachers should not bargain or strike.

This antibargaining argument actually grew out of organizational rivalry between the NEA, which had prided itself on being a professional association, and the AFT, which stressed its status as a trade union affiliated with the AFL-CIO. In the early 1960s, AFT affiliates began urging collective bargaining seriously. More importantly from the NEA's point of view, AFT locals won virtually all the early representation elections, thereby establishing the AFT as a much more serious threat to the NEA. At the time the NEA was an all-inclusive association, that is, it enrolled school administrators as well as teachers as members. In attempting to maintain its organizational supremacy over the AFT, the NEA initially denounced collective bargaining as incompatible with the professional status of teachers.

The appeal to professionalism as an argument against teachers' bargaining or teachers' strikes did not last very long. On its own terms, the appeal left other public employees free to strike. When the issue was formulated as a choice between something called "professional status" and the right to strike, teachers opted for the right to strike. More importantly, however, the professionalism argument treated professionals (employed by a single employer (for example, teachers) as if they were fee takers. Fee takers such as doctors, dentists, and lawyers do not strike because they do not have a common employer. There is ordinarily no reason for them to withdraw their services collectively. On the other hand, where doctors, for example, are employed collectively by a single employer, as are public-school teachers, doctors strike as if they were nonprofessional employees. Or, if they do not, the reason is not that strikes are deemed unprofessional; it is rather that they are unnecessary because of the enormous bargaining power of doctors.

In any event, the NEA first approved professional negotiations in 1962. At that time it also approved the use of professional sanctions in certain situations. Nobody was sure what "professional sanctions" meant, which was their overriding value internally. They could be interpreted as inclusive of strikes, thereby satisfying members who wanted NEA to support the right to strike. At the same time "professional sanctions" could be interpreted to mean something much less than this, thereby satisfying the antistrike faction. These ambiguous resolutions launched NEA on a course of action that led to its all-out support of collective bargaining and the right to strike in less than ten years. To compete successfully with the AFT (which had adopted a resolution supporting the right to strike in 1964), the NEA had to proclaim itself and act like a union, which it did whenever and wherever organizational rivalry required such a stance. Understandably, administrators began leaving or getting pushed out of the NEA in large numbers in the middle 1960s. Their departure marked as well as accelerated the emergence of the NEA as a union. In the early 1960s the NEA had supported strikes but had labeled them "professional holidays" and/or "professional sanctions." Before long, the association was asserting that true professionals did not avoid strikes but supported them, all in the name of the children, of course. Thus when the resolution supporting the right to strike was adopted in 1968, it was more a change in terminology than a change in the basic policy of the association.

As a matter of fact, the circumstances of the NEA's conversion to collective bargaining were most unfortunate from a public-policy standpoint. NEA's rivalry with the AFT required NEA to espouse some form of organized representation at the local level. The difficulty was that the NEA could not embrace collective bargaining as that would mean embracing the policy urged by its rival union. It also would have required an extremely embarrassing policy reversal, certain to drive conservative teachers out of the association. Therefore, the NEA came out for professional negotiation instead of collective bargaining.

What was the difference between "collective bargaining" and "professional negotiations"? The NEA's response was that teachers were professionals, and professionals wanted to negotiate more than terms and conditions of employment. They wanted to negotiate or have the right to negotiate on everything that affected their work, which meant, of course, just about everything. Thus when the huge NEA organizational apparatus turned around, it did not merely change from an antibargainist to a bargainist position. It embraced the most extreme and indefensible position on the scope of bargaining, thereby greatly exacerbating actual bargaining conflicts at the local level. Thousands of teacher negotiators took seriously the view that "everything is negotiable," even when their leadership realized privately that such a position was probably as dangerous organizationally as it was indefensible politically.

The notion that professionals have the right to bargain on matters beyond the purview of other employees was not confined to education. In fact, a union of social workers in New York City, the Social Service Employees Union (SSEU), provided a dramatic example of the ultimate consequences of this position. After a long strike by the SSEU in 1965, New York City agreed contractually to consider all proposals submitted by the union in future negotiations. Spero and Capozzola describe what happened thereafter.

Henceforth, the SSEU made determined efforts to bargain on such policy matters as case standards, physical conditions, rental of new office space, facility refurbishing, and acquisition of computerized data-processing machinery, as well as training programs, caseloads of welfare workers, recruitment, selection, promotion, and hiring of reserve staffs in each welfare office to assist field investigators.

By 1967 the SSEU was not only insisting upon such items as a reduction of caseload but demanding that specific programs, such as the hiring of 500 new trainees per month, be written into the contract, guaranteeing that the program would be carried out. Still other demands incorporated the SSEU's conception of the meaning of "welfare," which was held to include the right to telephones for all clients and the right of clients to be allowed to keep the entire income from the first month of employment rather than take a commensurate reduction in their welfare grants.

The union also demanded that the Department of Welfare make down payments and pay maintenance charges so that clients might move into cooperative housing. Increased and automatic twice-a-year clothing allowances, improved facilities, Spanish-speaking interpreters, and the establishment of residential treatment centers were also sought. Each of the demands, said the SSEU, would lighten workloads, "streamline" working procedures, improve operations, and benefit the public as well as the client.

Astounded officials refused to bargain on many of the issues, the 1965 contract notwithstanding.[7]

Not surprisingly, another strike took place in 1967. Although an agreement was reached, the SSEU continued to resort to job actions to achieve its bargaining objectives. The city's position was succinctly stated by the commissioner of welfare: "We feel strongly that labor-management contracts cannot be the vehicle by which reform in public welfare is accomplished." By 1969 the SSEU was replaced as bargaining agent by AFSCME, which had lost the representation election to the SSEU in 1964. In short, the greatest danger of the professional view that "everything is negotiable" is that the public employees themselves may take this view seriously. In doing so, they overlook the antidemocratic implications of the position that all public policies must be negotiated with one special-interest group.

The Erosion of the Prohibition
against Public-Sector Strikes

The changing policy toward strikes in the NEA was typical of public-sector unions in the 1960s. Virtually all the national unions representing public employees, as well as several state civil-service-type associations, formally repeated their no-strike policies and adopted resolutions asserting the legitimacy of strikes by public employees. The following list is illustrative:

Year in which No-Strike Policy Was Repealed	Association or Union
1964	American Federation of Teachers, AFL-CIO
1966	American Federation of State, County, and Municipal Employees, AFL-CIO
1967	New York State Civil Service Employees Association
1968	National Education Association
1968	International Association of Fire-Fighters, AFL-CIO
1968	American Nursing Association
1970	AFSCME (for Police Affiliates)

Many of the repealed no-strike policies had been in effect for decades prior to repeal. In fact, it appears that virtually all major national unions representing public employees renounced the resort to strikes prior to 1960. These renunciations usually stated that the unions did not favor the use of strikes or they believed that strikes should be unnecessary. They were not precisely condemnations of strikes as inherently unjustified or illegal; hence it was not difficult for unions to assert the legitimacy of strikes.

The changes in union attitudes were both cause and result of the dramatic increase in public-sector strikes beginning in the early 1960s. Table 2-1 shows this increase was clearly associated with increases in bargaining statutes and membership in public-sector labor organizations. Table 2-2 relates the numbers of strikes in 1972 and 1977 to levels and type of governments; table 2-3 shows the incidence of strikes in functional categories of employees. The differences between table 2-1 and tables 2-2 and 2-3 on the total number of strikes in 1972 and 1977 appear to be due to the use of different beginning and ending dates for the reporting year.

When public employees strike, other public employees in the same area are interested observers. If they see that a strike is successful—or that it does not result in any dire consequences to the strikers—they have an incentive to strike also. Thus if police unions strike and achieve gains, unions of firefighters are more likely to do so. In effect, the number and outcome of public-sector strikes in the 1960s reached a sort of critical mass, after which it became politically imperative for union leadership to espouse the right to strike.

Table 2-1
Public-Sector Strikes, 1958-1978

Year	States with Bargaining Legislation	Public-Sector Union and Association Membership[a]	Number of Strikes
1958	0	1,035,000	15
1959	1	—	25
1960	1	1,070,000	36
1961	2	—	28
1962	2	1,225,000	28
1963	2	—	29
1964	2	1,453,000	41
1965	9	—	42
1966	10	1,717,000	142
1967	13	—	181
1968[b]	15	3,857,000	254
1969	23	—	411
1970	28	4,080,000	412
1971	30	—	329
1972	31	4,520,000	375
1973	34	—	387
1974	36	5,345,000	384
1975	36	—	478
1976	36	5,852,000	378
1977	36	—	413
1978	37	6,019,000	481[c]

Source: Public Service Research Council, *Public Sector Bargaining and Strikes*, 4th ed. (Vienna, Va.: Public Service Research Council, 1980), p. 5.

[a]Data on public-sector union and association membership compiled by the Bureau of Labor Statistics biannually.

[b]Data on public-sector association membership only available since 1968.

[c]Preliminary figure from BLS.

Given the increasing number of public employees and their growing political influence, it is not surprising that cracks in the legislative wall against public-sector strikes began to appear. In 1969 Vermont legitimized teacher strikes, and Montana legitimized strikes by publicly employed nurses. In 1970 Hawaii and Pennsylvania legalized strikes by most public employees. By 1979 eight states (Alaska, Hawaii, Minnesota, Montana, Oregon, Pennsylvania, Vermont, and Wisconsin) had enacted a right to strike for at least some public employees. Typically the right was conditional on completion of a state-mandated impasse procedure without an agreement and excluded police and firefighters, but the position that public employees should have the right to strike could no longer be dismissed as rare or extremist.

In and of itself, union support for legalizing public-employee strikes was probably insufficient to persuade legislatures to do so. Another key fac-

Table 2-2
State and Local Government Work Stoppages by Level and Type of Government

| Level and Type of Government | Number of Work Stoppages | | Employees Involved | | | | Duration (Days) | | | | Days of Idleness (Employees × Days) | | | |
| | | | Total | | Average per Stoppage | | Total | | Average per Stoppage | | Total | | Average per Stoppage | |
	1977	1972	1977	1972	1977	1972	1977	1972	1977	1972	1977	1972	1977	1972
Total	485	381	178,814	130,871	369	343	3,608	2,705	7.4	7.1	1,457,475	1,124,007	3,005.1	2,950.1
State governments	33	34	35,203	20,758	1,067	611	136	219	4.1	6.4	183,530	119,809	5,561.5	3,523.8
Local governments	452	347	143,611	110,113	318	317	3,472	2,486	7.7	7.2	1,273,945	1,004,198	2,818.5	2,893.9
Counties	61	31	18,907	8,338	310	269	557	218	9.1	7.0	96,527	49,444	1,582.4	1,595.0
Municipalities	154	133	26,646	29,459	173	222	1,072	761	11.1	5.7	174,870	176,336	1,135.5	1,325.8
Townships	20	9	3,163	1,433	158	159	95	59	4.8	6.6	16,697	12,408	834.9	1,378.7
Special districts	24	22	9,189	6,152	383	280	222	217	9.3	9.9	49,887	62,956	2,078.6	2,861.6
School districts	193	152	85,706	64,731	444	426	1,526	1,231	7.9	8.1	935,964	703,054	4,849.6	4,625.4

Table 2-3
State and Local Government Work Stoppages by Function

Function	Number of Work Stoppages		Employees Involved				Duration (Days)				Days of Idleness (Employees × Days)			
			Total		Average per Stoppage		Total		Average per Stoppage		Total		Average per Stoppage	
	1977	1972	1977	1972	1977	1972	1977	1972	1977	1972	1977	1972	1977	1972
Total	485	381	178,814	130,871	369	343	3,608	2,705	7.4	7.1	1,457,475	1,124,007	3,005.1	2,950.1
Education	225	193	98,398	90,256	437	469	2,436	1,552	10.8	8.0	1,056,300	888,027	4,694.7	4,601.2
Teachers	174	146	69,780	71,716	401	491	1,370	1,085	7.9	7.4	763,975	644,562	4,390.7	4,414.8
Other	131	95	28,614	18,810	218	198	1,066	894	8.1	9.4	292,325	243,465	2,231.5	2,562.8
Highways	58	58	4,167	3,336	72	58	539	379	9.3	6.5	25,233	22,710	435.1	391.6
Public welfare	13	11	8,607	2,526	662	230	114	48	8.8	4.4	21,599	15,187	1,661.5	1,380.1
Hospitals	20	16	9,447	11,054	472	691	176	138	8.8	8.6	53,553	39,949	2,677.7	2,496.8
Police protection	36	22	2,058	661	57	30	128	109	3.6	5.0	6,950	2,561	193.1	116.4
Fire protection	24	11	3,342	572	139	52	82	51	3.4	4.6	7,053	3,606	293.9	327.8
Sanitation	55	65	5,494	4,080	999	63	357	403	6.5	6.2	32,365	27,465	588.5	422.5

Source: Bureau of National Affairs, *Government Employee Relations Report*, Reference File—186 (Washington, D.C.: Bureau of National Affairs, 10 December 1979), p. 71:4095.

tor was the support for legalization from university experts on collective bargaining. Despite some exceptions such as the members of the Taylor Committee, and some differences regarding the conditions of legalization, the labor-relations community in higher education urged legalization. Such support made it much easier for public-sector unions and their leadership to advocate legalization; they could point to prestigious academics who agreed that such prohibitions were anachronistic or inequitable or otherwise undesirable. Furthermore, academics favoring legalization of strikes frequently served as consultants to legislative bodies and took an active role in conferences and training programs devoted to public-sector labor relations. Beyond question, academic support for legalization was (and is) a critical factor in the movement to legalize public-sector strikes.

When all is said and done, however, it must be recognized that public management, and especially the state and national organizations of public management, failed to recognize the far-reaching ramifications of public-sector strikes or the complex problems of enacting effective statutory prohibitions against strikes. For the most part, public management outside the South was more or less resigned to the enactment of public-sector bargaining. As a result, emphasis was placed on ensuring that strikes by public employees would be illegal. Unfortunately, at least from a managerial point of view, the mechanics and dynamics of public-sector strikes were not fully understood; hence many of the legislative prohibitions were not effective.

Preoccupation with making strikes illegal led to several legislative blunders by the antibargaining forces. First of all, they had no effective response to bargaining laws that made public-sector strikes illegal. Unfortunately, the number of strikes by public employees has increased in the bargaining-law states, even in those where the bargaining laws prohibit such strikes.[8] In the 1960s, however, this outcome was neither a matter of record nor so easily foreseen; hence the opponents of bargaining felt that they could only go along and hope for the best. To be candid, many public employers were persuaded that bargaining was only a procedural requirement, and they reasoned that if strikes were prohibited and if they did not agree with union proposals, all they had to do was stick to their positions until the impasse procedures were completed. At that point, the union would have to accept the employer's offer. What alternative would the union have if it could not strike? And seeing none, they were not as critical of other aspects of the proposed bargaining statutes as they might otherwise have been. By the time they realized the duration and costs of these procedural requirements and discovered that some of them were substantive as well, it was too late to block or undo the enactment of a bargaining statute.

Confronted by complex legislative proposals, by policy analysis dominated by interest groups that stood to gain the most from bargaining statutes, and by inadequate data on most crucial issues, the legislatures responded in different ways to the essential-service argument, or the public-health-and-safety argument. Some legalized bargaining but prohibited strikes. Some legalized bargaining for some public employees, such as teachers, but not for others, such as police and firefighters. Some legalized strikes but provided for prompt injunctive relief if public health or safety was threatened by a strike. In other words, the argument that bargaining would lead to strikes was often successful in bringing about changes in proposed bargaining legislation, but it was not successful in blocking such legislation altogether.

The Effectiveness of Strike Prohibitions

The data on strikes by public employees and the controversies over these data raise several troublesome questions. For instance, one frequently encounters the view that public employees strike even if such strikes are illegal; therefore, the best thing to do is not engage in a futile effort to prohibit strikes but seek to eliminate their causes and control their incidence.

Persons will rob and murder despite laws prohibiting theft and murder. Therefore we should not prohibit theft and murder but seek to eliminate their causes and regulate their incidence. Most readers would regard this argument as absurd, and rightly so. We do not expect legal prohibitions to be completely successful, nor do we regard occasional violations as evidence of the futility of the prohibitions. By the same token, the argument for legalizing strikes, on the basis that strikes occur even in the face of legal prohibitions, fails to differentiate the kinds of legal prohibitions that are effective from those that are not.

Arguably, the illegality of strikes per se does not have a significant impact on their incidence. The evidence to be discussed shortly clearly suggests that it does, but for the sake of argument, let us waive the point. The crucial point is not that some legal prohibitions are ineffective but that some are effective. This being the case, it hardly makes sense to emphasize the high incidence of strikes under ineffective prohibitions and to conclude that it is futile to attempt to prohibit public-sector strikes.

In addition, those who support legalization of strikes typically ignore this question: Granted that strikes will sometimes occur where they are statutorily prohibited, do statutory prohibitions result in fewer strikes than would occur if strikes were legalized?

The answer is clear: More strikes would occur in the same jurisdiction if strikes were legalized. As one example, almost one fifth of all the public-sector strikes in the United States have occurred in Pennsylvania since that state legalized public-sector strikes in 1970. Prior to legalization, Pennsylvania experienced about 6 public-sector strikes a year; after legalization in 1970, the state averaged 78 strikes annually from 1971 to 1977. Significantly, among the states that statutorily prohibit public-sector strikes, New York, which ranks sixth in the incidence of strikes among all states, has had the most. Nevertheless, it has far fewer than Pennsylvania, which has legalized strikes, and significantly fewer than Ohio, Michigan, California, and Illinois, which have only judicial prohibitions against them. Furthermore, if anything is clear, it is that the public-employee unions in New York do not regard the statutory prohibitions as ineffective. On the contrary, elimination of the statutory prohibitions, or reduction of the statutory penalties for striking, has been a major legislative objective of public-sector unions in New York since the enactment of that state's bargaining statute in 1967.[9] These efforts would be incomprehensible if the penalties had as little practical effect as some analysts assert.

In practice, the effectiveness of a prohibition against public-sector strikes depends on several factors, but especially on whether the provisions for enforcement are judicial or statutory.

To the layman, if something is illegal, the source of the illegality is not important. To lawyers, public employers, and public-employee unions, however, what makes a public-employee strike illegal is crucially important. If a strike is illegal as a result of judicial decisions (as distinguished from being illegal pursuant to a statute), the problems of enforcement can be all but insuperable in the short run—and most strikes do not last beyond the short run. The public employer must go into court, seeking a temporary restraining order against the strike. A temporary restraining order is issued only if the requesting party can show (1) irreparable damage if not granted the order, and (2) the likelihood that the request will be sustained on its merits at a later date, and (3) "clean hands," that is, the public employer must not have done anything that would justify denial of equitable relief. The strikers, especially the union leaders, must be served with notice of the hearing, a requirement that is often easier said than done. The public employer must find a judge willing to hold a hearing promptly and rule favorably on the petition for a temporary restraining order. These are only a few of the problems, many of which require a substantial amount of time when maximum effort must be made to maintaining public services.

Sometimes successful enforcement of a temporary restraining order presents public employers with more difficult problems than the strike itself. Jail sentences for contempt may make heroes out of strike leaders (at least in the eyes of their constituents); the demand for amnesty may itself become a highly controversial issue. In the context of a settlement, public employers may be willing to forgive and forget—to the angry dismay of the judges who issued the temporary restraining orders. And where public employers fail to enforce penalties against strikers, the latter are naturally encouraged to use the strike again.[10]

Strike prohibitions can be ineffective for several other reasons. The penalties may be so severe that public officials lose public support by invoking them. Or it may be practically impossible to invoke the penalties; for example, in states where school boards must still follow the state tenure law, it is virtually impossible to fire teachers who strike. The tenure laws were enacted with individual cases in mind. Nobody thought of tenure laws as relevant to strikes by public employees, partly because of the widespread belief and legal decisions that such strikes were illegal as a matter of common law. Indeed, some state bargaining laws said nothing either way about the legality of public-sector strikes. This usually happened when the public-employee unions successfully excluded a prohibition against strikes on the grounds that they were illegal by court decision, that is, by common-law principles. It was thus argued that a legislative prohibition was unnecessary. Legislators caught between public-employee unions and public-management organizations sometimes took this way out. To the unions, they could say that they had not insisted on a no-strike provision in the bargaining statute. To public officials, they could point to the fact—or alleged fact—that public-employee strikes were illegal by court decision even in the absence of statute.

California: A Case Study of Management Failure

California is a showcase example of how public management failed to respond effectively to public-sector-bargaining legislation. In early 1975 Senator Albert Rodda introduced a bill that provided bargaining rights for school-district employees. Despite the fact that they could have killed any collective-bargaining legislation, the California School Boards Association (CSBA) and the Association of California School Administrators (ACSA) actively supported this bill. They did so even though the bill:

1. Did not prohibit strikes by school-district employees.
2. Accorded bargaining rights to supervisors; under the National Labor Relations Act, supervisors have not had bargaining rights since 1948.
3. Mandated "a reasonable amount" of released time with pay for bargaining and for processing grievances. In conjunction with the lengthy impasse procedures, requiring public employers to provide employees time off with pay to negotiate was certain to prolong bargaining, as indeed has been the case.
4. Provided that there can be no diminution through bargaining of the tremendous number of employee benefits already provided statutorily for school-district employees. In no other state was public-sector bargaining superimposed over a higher level of irreducible benefits for public employees.

5. Authorized employee organizations to represent their members on matters within the scope of representation even if the organizations failed to win exclusive recognition. Thus it was futile for public employers to conduct a "no-representation" campaign since they had to deal with the union anyway.

6. Required school boards to accord unions several rights and privileges that elsewhere are achieved by unions through bargaining, if they are achieved at all. Employers who agree to such rights and privileges as a result of bargaining can get union concessions as a quid pro quo. By providing these rights statutorily, the Rodda Act precluded such an outcome.

7. Required school employers to negotiate only with representatives of unions designated as exclusive representatives but imposed no corresponding obligation on the union to negotiate only with representatives of employers. This omission predictably encouraged unions to negotiate or try to negotiate with individual school-board members for a better deal than was being offered at the table by the board's negotiator.

8. Forced school boards to negotiate long before they knew their state-aid revenues, which now constitute over 80 percent of district revenues. Thus the law requires months of fruitless and pointless negotiations, with the school districts paying for the time of representatives on both sides of the table.

As enacted, the Rodda Act did not include a prohibition of strikes. The management organizations (ASCA and CSBA) accepted the argument that such a prohibition was unnecessary in view of several decisions by state courts holding that public-employee strikes were illegal as a matter of common law. This deference to a prior judicial resolution of the issue turned out to be disastrous.

In a 1979 decision related to a strike by San Diego teachers, the California Supreme Court held that school boards did not have standing to enjoin strikes that might be unfair labor practices.[11] The specific issue before the court was whether the Superior Court of San Diego County had jurisdiction to issue a temporary restraining order (TRO) against a strike by San Diego teachers. In a 4-3 decision that it did not, the California Supreme Court reasoned as follows:

1. Section 3541.5 of the Rodda Act provides that "the initial determination as to whether the charges of unfair practices are justified, and if so, what remedy is necessary to effectuate the purposes of this chapter, shall be a matter within the exclusive jurisdiction of the board" (that is, the state PERB).

2. A strike prior to completion of the statutory impasse procedures was arguably an unfair labor practice; hence only the PERB had jurisdiction to seek a TRO against the striking teachers.

Inasmuch as the TRO issued by the Superior Court was not based on a request by the PERB, it was null and void, as were the penalties against the teachers for violating the order.

As a result of the San Diego decision, school boards seeking to enjoin strikes had to persuade the state PERB to request the TRO in a state court. Unfortunately, there was no statutory or judicial requirement that the PERB act promptly on such requests. In view of the fact that two of the three members of the PERB were on record as supporting the legalization of strikes, school boards could hardly expect prompt support for their requests that the PERB seek to enjoin strikes by district employees. Inasmuch as most public-employee strikes do not last more than a few days, the practical effect of the San Diego decision was to legalize strikes until the PERB was successful in enjoining them.

Actually, the San Diego decision was more harmful than an outright statutory legalization of strikes would have been. The decision held that a strike prior to completion of the impasse procedures might be an unfair labor practice. The unions sought to counter this by alleging that the school employers were not negotiating in good faith, that is, that they were committing unfair labor practices of their own. Such charges by the union ran the risk of being viewed as formalities, intended to excuse the union's conduct. To avoid this interpretation, unions filed charges of unfair labor practices against school districts before going on strike. In other words, the San Diego decision encouraged unions to file unfair-labor-practice charges to provide credibility to their claims that their strikes were provoked by the unfair labor practices of the school districts. While the labor lawyers made out like bandits, district after district was subjected to a barrage of unfair-labor-practice charges, accompanied if not orchestrated with maximum media exposure. The final twist of the screw took place in the spring of 1980 when the PERB took the position that it maintained jurisdiction over strikes even after the impasse procedures were exhausted.[12] This position was upheld by the California lower courts.

One reason ACSA and CSBA supported the Rodda Act was that it appeared to provide a narrow scope of negotiations. Thus part of the legislative bargain that culminated in the act was the following provision on the scope of negotiations:

3543.2. The scope of representation shall be limited to matters relating to wages, hours of employment, and other terms and conditions of employment. "Terms and conditions of employment" mean health and welfare benefits . . . leave and transfer policies, safety conditions of employment, class size, procedures to be used for the evaluation of employees, organizational security . . . and procedures for processing grievances . . . All matters not specifically enumerated are reserved to the public school employer and may not be a subject of meeting and negotiatng, provided that nothing herein may be construed to limit the right of the public school employer to consult with any employees or employee organization on any matter outside the scope of representation.

As so often happens, what a legislature does is one matter and how it is administratively interpreted and implemented is another. Thus in June 1980 the state PERB issued decisions in two lengthy scope-of-negotiation cases.[13] In effect, the decisions interpreted section 3543.2 of the Rodda Act as providing a scope of negotiations virtually identical to the private sector; as a matter of fact, a dissenting member of the PERB specifically asserted this conclusion, which is shared by virtually all management and union representatives in the state.

In any event, in less than six years, the following sequence of events had occurred in California:

1. Court decisions held that public-employee strikes are illegal as a matter of common law.
2. A public-employee bargaining law was enacted without a no-strike clause on the basis that such strikes are prohibited as a matter of common law.
3. Without a single vote in the legislature, California was transformed from being a state in which strikes by school-district employees were illegal to a state in which the legality of such strikes is, for all practical purposes, a discretionary matter with a state administrative agency that is aggressively asserting and promoting the legality of strikes by school-district employees.

How did California school districts get into this situation? Incredibly, neither ACSA or CSBA employed labor-relations counsel expert in collective bargaining for a critical analysis of the Rodda Act before it was enacted. When the consequences of the act began to dawn on California school administrators, ACSA officers explained their support for it by saying such support was necessary to head off a more harmful law. This was not true, but the state's school administrators, lacking access to the legislative situation, accepted the explanation and set about trying to cope with the law.[14]

On the school-board side, the story took a different turn. CSBA fired its executive director, but a more pleasant fate awaited the attorney who drafted the Rodda Act. He had graduated from law school in 1974, and was admitted to practice that year. From 1965 to 1974, he had been employed in student personnel administration at the University of California-Davis; from 1973-1976, he served as associate consultant to the California Senate Education Committee. In this capacity, this neophyte attorney worked for Senator Rodda, an ardent unionist who was committee chairman, and drafted the legislation that brought collective bargaining to California's $11 billion public-school system. The year after the Rodda Act was enacted, he joined the law firm that served as labor-relations counsel for CSBA. CSBA's law firm added his name to the firm title, and the firm is now one of California's largest in the field of school-district labor relations. Understandably, neither it nor its client school-board association appears to be a promising source of leadership in achieving reform of the Rodda Act.

Notes

1. Most notably, by Robert S. Summers, *Collective Bargaining and Public Benefit Conferral: A Jurisprudential Critique*, IPE Monograph No. 7 (Ithaca, N.Y.: Institute of Public Employment, Cornell University, November 1976); and Robert S. Summers, "Public Sector Bargaining Substantially Diminishes Democracy," *Government Union Review* (Winter 1980):5-22.

2. See David Ziskind, *One Thousand Strikes of Government Workers* (New York: Columbia University Press, 1940).

3. Assembly Advisory Council on Public Employee Relations, *Final Report and Proposed Statute of the California Assembly Advisory Council on Public Employee Relations* (Sacramento, Calif.: Speaker of the Assembly, State Capitol, State of California, 15 March 1973), pp. 229-230. Examples of earlier advocacy of a public-sector right to strike may be found in Myron Lieberman, "Teachers' Strikes: An Analysis of the Issues," *Harvard Educational Review* 26 (Winter 1956):39-70; and John F. Burton, Jr., and Charles Krider, "The Role and Consequences of Strikes by Public Employees," in *Collective Bargaining in Government: Readings and Cases*, eds., J. Joseph Loewenberg and Michael H. Moskow (Englewood Cliffs, N.J.: Prentice-Hall, 1972), pp. 247-288.

4. Governor's Committee on Public Employee Relations, *Final Report* (Albany, N.Y.: State of New York, 31 March 1966), pp. 39-44.

5. For a caustic analysis of the sovereignty argument as a rationale for prohibiting public-sector strikes, see Sterling D. Spero and John Capozzola, *The Urban Community and Its Unionized Bureaucracies* (New York: Dunellen Publishing, 1972), pp. 265-266.

6. For an early criticism of the essential-service rationale for prohibiting strikes by all public employees, see Lieberman, "Teachers'

Strikes,'' pp. 39-70. Academic advocacy of liberalization of public-employee rights to strike has continued to the late 1970s; see, for example, David Lewin, Raymond D. Horton, and James W. Kuhn, *Collective Bargaining and Manpower Utilization in Big City Governments* (New York: Universe Books, 1979), pp. 134-138.

7. See Spero and Capozzola, *The Urban Community*, pp. 179-182, for an account of developments related to the SSEU.

8. See also *Public Sector Bargaining and Strikes* (Vienna, Va.: Public Service Research Council, 1980), pp. 1-21.

9. For an account of union efforts to eliminate the statutory penalties for striking in New York, see the *Government Union Critique* 2 (23 May 1980):1-2.

10. An excellent analysis of the problems of enforcing a judicial prohibition of public-sector strikes may be found in David L. Colton and Edith E. Graber, *Enjoining Teacher Strikes: The Irreparable Harm Standard* (St. Louis: Center for the Study of Law in Education, Washington University, 1980).

11. *San Diego Teachers Association* v. *Superior Court of San Diego County* (1979) 24 Cal. 3d 1.

12. See *Modesto Teachers Association* v. *Modesto City Schools*, PERB Decision No. IR 12, 12 March 1980.

13. *California School Employees Association* v. *Healdsburg Union High School District and Healdsburg Union School District*, PERB Decision 132, June 19, 1980; and *Jefferson Classroom Teachers Association, CTA/NEA* v. *Jefferson School District*, PERB Decision 133, June 19, 1980.

14. A letter and enclosures from Senator Rodda to the author, dated 16 March 1976, makes it clear that ACSA and CSBA actively supported the Rodda Act and that there would have been no bargaining legislation affecting school districts during the 1975 session of the legislature without their support.

3 Bargaining Rights as Equity for Public Employees

The most important and most persuasive argument for public-sector bargaining was and is the equity argument. The argument is that public employees are second-class citizens because they do not have the rights to bargain and to strike as employees do in the private sector. Supporters of this argument frequently propose that public employees be accorded the same rights to bargain and to strike as exist in the private sector. The executive director of the NEA recently advocated this proposal in the following way:

> At the outset, astute observers perceived that the private sector collective bargaining experience was relevant and offered a ready-made, comprehensive, well-understood, and adequately tested model for conflict resolution. It had respected the interest of employees and employers and had provided stability in production and commerce.
>
> The model was built on the concept of equalizing the power of the employee and the employer through a system that provided
>
> > the protected right to organize
> >
> > the employer's obligation to recognize the employee's chosen union as the exclusive bargaining agent
> >
> > the obligation to bargain in good faith
> >
> > an independent enforcement agency
> >
> > fair impasse resolution machinery
> >
> > the right to strike
> >
> > a written, enforceable collective bargaining contract.
>
> Each element contributed to the success of the model and, to the extent that it has been tried, has been useful in the public sector. Nevertheless, policy for the public sector invariably hedges some or all bets. . . .
>
> It is clear, nevertheless, that a comprehensive public sector labor policy based upon the private sector system is valid. The closer it hews to the private sector system, the more positive is the result. The further it departs from that system, the less it fulfills its intended purpose of conflict management. The public sector system currently in existence often departs from the private sector model in critical areas. In perpetuating these differences, state legislatures are saying implicitly that they are not really trying to manage conflict but only to finesse it. The point is not lost on public employees. They understand full well that where no system exists, the legislature has left the conflict to its own course, wherever it leads.[1]

One problem with this argument is that the rights of private-sector unions are highly controversial matters in our society. Both what are and what should be the legal rights of private-sector unions are matters of widespread dispute, and both law and public opinion in this area have changed and are changing. An individual may believe that both private and public-sector unions should have more rights than they do. To such an individual, the equity argument would be irrelevant. The individual might support according public-sector unions certain rights not currently enjoyed by private ones, simply on the basis that it is better to provide as many unions as possible with their rights.

By the same token, another individual may believe that private-sector unions have too many rights now. Such an individual might believe in achieving equity by reducing the rights of private-sector unions instead of increasing the rights of public-sector ones. This analysis does not take sides, or have any opinion to offer, on the legitimate rights of private-sector unions. The intent here is simply to note that the argument for public-employee bargaining rights, insofar as it is based on equity with private-sector employees, may be based on an assumption about private-sector bargaining rights that is open to both challenge and change.

The appeal to equal treatment under the law has always been a powerful one in our history and especially in the last two decades. For this reason, the fact that public employees do not have rights accorded employees in the private sector undeniably exercises a strong appeal to voters and legislators.

In the 1960s the appeal to equity was perhaps *the* major public-policy justification for public-sector bargaining. Without bargaining rights, public employees are allegedly second-class citizens. Privately employed guards can unionize and strike; publicly employed ones cannot. Bus drivers for a privately owned company can strike; if the same routes were taken over and operated as a public utility, the drivers could not bargain or strike. Similarly, teachers in private schools can organize and bargain; those in public schools cannot.

It should be noted that in some of these examples, the same employees would or would not have the right to strike, depending on whether they were private- or public-sector employees. For instance, school-bus drivers employed by a private company with a contract to transport children have the right to bargain collectively and to strike. If those same bus drivers were employed by the school district, they would not have the right to bargain collectively and to strike in the absence of a bargaining law. Similarly, sanitation workers employed privately can bargain collectively and strike; municipal employees doing exactly the same job could not bargain collectively and strike without statutory authorization.[2]

These examples show why the equity argument had a particularly strong appeal. They suggest that only a technicality or legal nicety prevents public-sector employees from bargaining and/or striking if they so desire. In these cases at least, the impact of bargaining and strikes on the public appears to be identical. For this reason, the argument that bargaining and strikes by public employees would lead to disaster seems weak, even hypocritical. If the impact on the public would be the same regardless of whether the employees were public or private, their rights to self-help ought to be the same.

Such was the argument, and it was undeniably effective. Of course, bargaining supporters frequently pushed the argument beyond its limits. For example, it was contended that since private-sector guards could bargain and strike, publicly employed security personnel such as police or fire-fighters, should also have the right. Pressed to this point, the analogy broke down and was intellectually shabby at best because the difference in numbers is crucial. To argue that a municipality can permit police to bargain and strike because private-sector guards can do so is fallacious; the consequences of these two strikes would not be substantially the same, even if there were a small overlap between the services.

For the sake of argument, let us agree that public employees ought to have equity with private-sector ones. To assess the equity argument objectively, however, we must consider all the significant differences between public and private employment, not just the absence of bargaining rights in the public sector. Public employees may lack certain rights and advantages available to private-sector employees; at the same time, however, the former may have other rights and advantages that private-sector employees do not enjoy. If this is the case, the equity argument for according public employees bargaining and strike rights may be weakened or even invalidated, depending on the extent of these rights and advantages.

The Advantages of Public Employment

Beyond any doubt, public employees do have certain rights and advantages not shared by private employees. In what follows, I have tried to summarize the most important ones. Subsequently, I shall cite some additional disadvantages of public employees before again addressing the equity issue on a comprehensive basis.

One major advantage of public over private employment is that public employees are entitled to certain employment rights even in the absence of a collective agreement or statutory protection. The principles involved (discussed in chapter 6) were set forth in a landmark case in which the U.S. Supreme Court held that public employees employed year after year may acquire a "property interest" in their jobs.[3] Once having acquired this interest—perhaps but not necessarily by the mere fact that they have been reappointed to the position for a period of time—they may not be deprived of it without due process of law. Due process of law is an elusive concept, but in this context, it can be interpreted to mean that the public employer must have a good reason to deprive employees of their jobs or of the major benefits or perquisites traditionally associated with it. Due process also includes basic procedural safeguards so that public employees have a reasonable opportunity to rebut the public employer's rationale for depriving the latter of their property interest in their employment. Thus public employees without bargaining rights frequently have more protection against arbitrary and unjust employer action than do private-sector employees with bargaining rights. Furthermore, this protection is grounded in the federal Constitution, not in any federal or state statute; thus the advantage of the public employee is a formidable one.

Another important advantage public employees have is their opportunity through the political process to play an important role in determining who is management. In contrast, private-sector employees have no legal or practical role in selecting management, and it would ordinarily be futile for them to try to do so.

In some jurisdictions at least, the political influence of public employees on public management has been extremely advantageous to the employees. This influence affects not only what is proposed, accepted, rejected, and modified in bargaining but the timing of concessions, the management posture toward grievances, and the extent of management support services for bargaining. Sometimes even the choice of management negotiator is subject to an unofficial but effective union veto.

There is a wealth of evidence that municipal unions wield substantial political power in large cities and that their political influence is reflected in generous agreements at the bargaining table. For example, one investigator recently concluded that the public-employee unions have replaced the political machine as the dominant force in Chicago's municipal government.[4] And it is of some interest and relevance that many informed observers of New York City's financial troubles regard excessive union contracts as the most important factor leading to the city's precarious financial condition.[5]

It is easy to underestimate the political influence of public employees. Typically, this influence has to be shared. Often it is more veto power than "do" power. One should not be misled, however, by the fact that candidates supported by public employees do not support the employees on each and every issue—or even oppose them on occasion. Such situations notwithstanding, the fact is that public employees can and often do play a decisive role in the determination of who makes the critical employer decisions in the bargaining process. Generally speaking, the larger the community, the more likely it is that this advantage of public employees will be operative, with or without bargaining.

In this connection, public-employee opportunities to influence the choice of state officials must also be considered. True enough, private-sector employees have equal opportunities to influence or to elect such officials. The point is, however, that elected state officials seldom affect the context or substance of private-sector bargaining. Typically, the governor of a state has no role in collective bargaining for private-sector employees. Such bargaining is regulated by the National Labor Relations Board, a federal agency. On the other hand, the governor frequently plays a decisive role in whether there is to be public-sector bargaining at all, and if there is, on such matters as the scope of bargaining, the nature of unfair labor practices, the relationship of bargaining to budgetary schedules, the impasse procedures, and the balance of bargaining power between the parties. In addition, governors often play a crucial role in substantive matters subject to bargaining. For example, the governor typically is the most important single individual in the annual aid-to-education controversy. Since states provide nearly half of school-district revenues, the gubernatorial role is much more important to school-district employees than it is to most private-sector unions. For school-district employees, the implications are obvious. Political activity pays them, as it does public employees generally, a larger dividend than it does the factory worker or the farmer. As a public-employee union leaflet states,

> AFSCME's Constitution points out that: "For unions, the work place and the polling place are inseparable. . . ." Public employees—more than any other group—know that their well-being and the quality of the services they perform are strongly affected by who holds public office.[6]

Equity and the Statutory Benefits of Public Employees

As previously noted, some of the advantages of public employment result from the fact that the Constitution restricts government as an employer in ways that do not apply to private employers. In addition, however, public employees often enjoy statutory benefits that exceed negotiated benefits in the private sector. The nature and extent of these statutory benefits varies widely from state to state. Also, even within states the benefits often vary widely from one category of public employees to another. Paradoxically, however, bargaining has emerged first and foremost in the states with the most statutory benefits for public employees and has yet to emerge in many states with minimal statutory benefits. Thus Mississippi has no bargaining law and minimal statutory benefits for public employees. On the other hand, California provides bargaining rights for school-district employees in addition to the following statutory benefits for teachers:

1. Strong protection against dismissal or suspension
2. Ten days of sick leave, cumulative without limit
3. Right to due process even as probationary employees
4. Substantial notice before termination
5. Layoff rights
6. Military, bereavement, personal necessity, legislative, industrial accident, and illness leaves
7. Sweeping protections in evaluation
8. Limits on district authority to reduce benefits
9. Protection against noncertified employees doing teacher work
10. Duty-free lunch periods
11. Right to dues deduction
12. Right to prompt payment of salary
13. Right to notice of school closing
14. Protection from legal actions for acts in the course of employment
15. Protection from being upbraided, insulted, or abused in the presence of pupils
16. Limits on the work day and work year

The preceding list is not exhaustive, but it is exceeded, if anything, by the statutory benefits provided nonteaching employees in California school districts. These benefits are so extensive and so complex that even a summary would not do them justice.[7] Their interpretation and application has become an arcane science, controlled largely by a handful of attorneys and union representatives who assume, usually correctly, that no one else has the patience to decode them.

There does not appear to be a single comprehensive summary of statutory benefits for public employees. There are, however, summaries of specific employee benefits, especially in the field of education, and they reveal an impressive array of statutory benefits and protections for public employees.[8] These studies reveal that as of 1975, all states had provisions for retirement benefits, almost all provided sick-leave benefits, 41 had teacher-tenure laws; 28 had provisions for sabbatical leave; 23 had limits on class size or pupil load, 43 regulated in some way the pupil day or pupil year (thus indirectly regulating teacher hours); and so on. Provisions relating to layoff rights, evaluation procedures, leaves of absence, duty-free lunch periods, and a host of other terms and conditions were frequent if not common. It is likely that other kinds of public employees also have substantial if somewhat different statutory benefits.

In the private sector, collective bargaining is the procedure to achieve employee benefits. Unions presumably have to make various concessions to get them if they get them at all; bargaining rights were not superimposed on a statutory system of fringe benefits. In the bargaining-law states, however, the statutory fringe benefits existed prior to bargaining, and no bargaining concession was required to achieve them. Providing bargaining rights in addition to these statutory benefits is not equity for public employees; it is more than equity by a wide margin.

Theoretically, the bargaining-law states could repeal all the statutory benefits for public employees, and the public employees could bargain from ground zero. For this reason, it may be argued that the existence of statutory benefits for public employees does not constitute an inherent advantage of public-sector over private-sector employees. In fact, however, even the legal possibilities are not so clear. In some states such as New York, public-employee pension benefits may not constitutionally be reduced for current participants. Unfortunately, this fact did not seem to lessen the generosity of the legislatures, which must now grapple with the problem of funding public-employee pension and retirement benefits that require alarming proportions of state revenues.

From a bargaining point of view, the legal status of employee benefits clearly presents an advantage to public employees. Once government provides a benefit, at least for as long as it takes to give the employees a property interest in it, government cannot deprive employees of the benefit without due process of law. This constitutes an enormous advantage of public employment. In the private sector, it is always difficult to take away employee benefits through the bargaining process. Unions are not in business to reduce but to add to benefits. The point is, however, that there is no *constitutional* problem to "takeaways." They present a bargaining problem, not a constitutional one, and then only if a union is involved. In the public sector, however, takeaways present basic constitutional problems. The full range of these problems is not clear at this time because of uncertainties related to the relevant Supreme Court decisions; nevertheless, public employees clearly have significant protections in the absence of bargaining that frequently exceed the protections of private-sector employees with bargaining rights.

The state bargaining laws fall into one of three categories with respect to other statutes on terms and conditions of public employment:

1. Some provide that nothing in the bargaining statute can supersede other statutes on terms and conditions of public employment.
2. Some provide that the terms of a negotiated agreement supersede any conflicting statute.
3. Some provide no legislative guidance on the issue.[9]

These courses of action will be discussed at length in chapter 6; here, our concern is only with the equity dimension of the options. Prima facie it appears that an extensive system of statutory as well as contractual benefits provides public employees with a significant advantage over private-sector employees. On the other hand, one can make the following argument for a dual system of benefits: Public employees have not had bargaining rights until the enactment of this law. If they had enjoyed bargaining rights, they would have contracts which included benefits bargained for over the years. Instead, they have been forced to achieve benefits legislatively. It would be unfair to take away the legislative benefits and force the public employees to start from ground zero in both bargaining and statutory benefits.

The argument has merit. Fundamentally, however, it has one major weakness. If public employees had had to bargain instead of lobby over the years, their fringe benefits would have been reflected in collective-bargaining contracts. As contractual benefits, they would be subject to diminution or even extinction through the bargaining process. Theoretically, it was possible to achieve such a transformation of statutory into contractual benefits, and the result would have been much more consistent with a comprehensive view of equity and the rationale for bargaining. Had the legislatures insisted on such a broad view of equity, it is anyone's guess as to what might have happened; beyond question, a substantial number of public employees who supported collective bargaining solely as an addition to their rights would have opposed it if it required giving up some rights not available to private-sector employees who bargain.

Bargaining Advantages and Disadvantages of Public-Sector Unions

The appeal to equity to justify public-sector bargaining actually raises two related but very different issues. One is whether, all things considered, public employees are disadvantaged procedurally in comparison to private-sector employees. The other issue is whether, assuming that an inequity exists, the establishment of public-sector bargaining rights is the appropriate way to achieve equity. One might believe that public employees are subject to an inequity but that a public-sector-bargaining law is not the appropriate way to remedy the inequity. For this reason, we must consider whether public-employee unions that bargain have any unique advantages or disadvantages in comparison to private-sector unions. The differential impact of the right to strike is perhaps the most important difference, but several others must be considered also.

In the private sector, the legal right to bargain and to strike has very different outcomes between industries, and often between companies in the same industry. First, most private-sector employees who have the legal right to bargain collectively do not do so. The reasons vary. In some fields, the task of organizing the employees and maintaining the necessary union cohesion is simply too difficult. For example, it is very difficult to organize household employees. There is widespread turnover, the number of employees is often too small to justify an organizing drive, the employer may be able to replace striking employees easily or even get by without them for a significant period of time, and so on. In other fields, the same set of legal rights leads to a much different result. For example, the transportation industry is highly unionized, and the Teamsters Union is an extremely powerful force in the industry. In some situations, a private-sector union has the power to cripple or even bankrupt an employer.[10]

Variations of this kind can and do exist under public-sector bargaining. With respect to some employees, the advent of bargaining rights changes very little, if anything. In other situations, these same rights provide public-employee unions with enormous influence over public services. In short, equality of procedural rights results in tremendous differences in bargaining power from situation to situation.

The differential impact of bargaining rights within each sector should not be allowed to obscure the fact that public-sector unions enjoy several advantages over private-sector unions in the bargaining process. The following discussion summarizes these advantages. The advantages do not necessarily apply to every private-sector situation. Nevertheless, they can be rightfully regarded as an advantage of public- over private-sector unions.

To illustrate, a public employer cannot move to another state or country to avoid unions and bargaining. This is clearly a bargaining advantage for public-employee unions. Obviously, moving is not a realistic alternative for some private-sector employers such as mining companies. As a practical matter, they may be as place-bound as public employers. Nevertheless, their inability to relocate is not inherent in private-sector bargaining per se. Instead, it is inherent in the nature of their particular enterprise. Similarly, the public-service union has important informational advantages over private-sector unions. Government budgets are public documents. Public-employee unions can easily determine past as well as present and projected expenditure patterns. Furthermore, they can be equally knowledgeable about comparison public agencies such as nearby police or fire departments. Again, it is not asserted that this advantage pertains to every private employer. Undoubtedly, there are situations in which the financial status and prospects of the private employer are as available to the union as are those of public employers. Nonetheless, an opportunity that, by its nature, is virtually always present in public-sector bargaining but varies widely in the private sector must be deemed an advantage of public-sector bargaining.

Of course, the practical value of the informational advantage varies. This is simply a recognition of the fact that the practical value of any advantage depends on the specific circumstances of each bargaining situation.

In general, public-employee unions are able to exert more pressure than private-sector unions on the employer. The reason they have this power is that public services tend to be monopolies that have no competitors, at least in the short run. A city cannot employ an adequate police or fire or sanitation department on short notice.

Most of the bargaining advantages—as well as the disadvantages—facing public-employee unions grow out of the political nature of public-sector bargaining. Fundamentally, such bargaining is over public policies. The policies can be categorized as personnel policies or as policies on terms and conditions of public employment—but they are public policies nonetheless. What we have, therefore, is not an economic test between private parties but a battle for public support between public employees on the one hand and public management on the other. A recognition of the political nature of public-sector bargaining is absolutely essential to understanding how and why it differs significantly from private-sector bargaining.

The political dimension of public-sector employment works to the advantage of public employees in several different ways. For example, there is greater turnover in the top echelons of public-sector management. More important, private-sector management tends to have a greater direct and personal stake in resisting unreasonable union demands. This is particularly apparent with respect to pension and retirement benefits. Public management sometimes achieves bargaining agreements by excessively generous pension and retirement benefits. Such concessions may not require any immediate tax increase. Thus the management officials responsible for the agreement can be heroes to the public employees for being generous and to the public for not raising taxes. Unfortunately, the practice saddles taxpayers with enormously expensive long-range commitments. Significantly, the tendency to "end-load" agreements this way has become evident in local, state, and federal governments. It is difficult to see the equity in requiring private-sector employees to provide retirement benefits for public employees that greatly exceed their own, but that is the present situation.

The crucial point is that public management has less incentive than private management to resist union demands. If private-sector management makes a concession that impairs the long-range profitability of the enterprise, that fact is reflected immediately in the value of the company. Thus, unlike public-sector management, private-sector management cannot avoid *immediate* accountability for agreeing to excessive deferred benefits. This reflects a significant bargaining advantage of public- over private-sector unions.

The individuals who negotiate and make the critical decisions for public management are affected politically, not economically by their actions. For instance, a businessman or a housewife on a school board is in a very different position from a contractor negotiating with construction unions or a vice-president for industrial relations responsible for bargaining with in-dustrial unions. Unlike private-sector management, the personal economic fortunes of school-board members are relatively independent of their ac-tions as public employers. Of course, political leaders in other areas of government may have an economic stake in their continuing role as political leaders; to that extent, the pressures on management in the two sectors are similar. Actually, the fact that individual public officials are not affected economically by their decisions as public employers sometimes results in a very hard bargaining line on their part. The public-sector unions have little leverage on public officials who are not subject to either political or economic pressure. In other situations, however, public officials often make concessions that they would never make as private-sector managers. On balance, however, it is difficult to say whether the differences in how management relates to bargaining outcomes is an advantage or disadvan-tage to public-sector unions.

Another advantage of public employees is that they have very little, if any, obligation of loyalty to their employer. On the other hand, private-sector employees are under some obligation not to damage the employer. In the context of a labor dispute, private-sector employees can urge the public not to purchase the employer's product or service, but otherwise their rights to criticize the employer's product or service are limited in ways that do not apply to public employees.

The leading private-sector case on this issue involved employees of a broadcasting company.[11] During a labor dispute, the employees, while still on the company payroll but on their off-duty hours, distributed handbills to the public critical of the station's programming. The handbills did not refer to the union or to an arbitration clause in dispute in the bargaining. In upholding the discharge of the employees for cause, the Court asserted, "There is no more elemental cause for discharge of an employee than disloyalty to his employer. . . . The legal principle that insubordination, disobedience, or disloyalty is adequate cause for discharge is plain enough."

In a subsequent case, the NLRB held that a paint-manufacturing com-pany was within its rights when it fired striking employees who distributed circulars alleging that the quality of the paint produced by their replacements might be inferior to the regular product.[12] Significantly, the employees were not on the payroll, referred to the labor dispute in the cir-cular, and stated that normal quality would return when the dispute was resolved.[13]

The obligation of loyalty to the employer in the private sector is virtu-ally absent in the public sector. Again, the reason is that when government acts as an employer, it is constrained constitutionally in ways that do not apply to private-sector employers. Public employees can (and often do) make damaging statements about public officials and public services. Their right to do so is protected by the First Amendment, and the Supreme Court has repeatedly held that a public employee may not be fired for exercising First Amendment rights.[14] Unless the public employer can show that the statements were maliciously false, it cannot take disciplinary action based on them.

In the Pickering case, a teacher wrote a letter to his local newspaper criticizing the board of education on the basis of several statements about the school budget that the Supreme Court conceded to be false. The Court nevertheless held that the board could not fire the teacher. In somewhat contradictory fashion, the Court asserted, "Teachers are as a class, the members of a community most likely to have informed and definite opinions as to how funds allotted to the operation of schools should be spent." It then excused the dismissed teacher's misstatements of fact on the basis that the actual amounts spent were matters of public record, on which the teacher had no more authority to speak than any other citizen! In any event, the Court's decision meant that a public employee could not be disciplined even for false statements if the statements were negligently rather than deliberately false. For that matter, a public employee could advocate the abolition of the public service that employs him and be fully protected in doing so. This is the way it should be; most emphatically, I am not advocating restrictions on public-employee rights to criticize public agencies. The point is, however, that public employees enjoy legal rights to criticize their employers and their employers' services and products that exceed such rights in the private sector. Needless to say, this is an advantage over private-sector employees, especially in view of the political dimension of public-sector bargaining.

As previously noted, the ability of public-sector unions to exert pressure on employers varies, as it does in the private sector. Unquestionably, the value of the strike, or the threat of a strike, also varies considerably in the public as well as the private sector. There are, however, a few factors that consistently render strikes by public employees more advantageous than strikes in the private sector. For instance, when the public-employee union strikes, it need not worry about the employer's moving, or going out of business, or losing business to competitors, or pricing itself out of the market. The exceptions and limitations to this statement hardly change its basic relevance and applicability. Certainly, there have been instances wherein a public agency discontinued a service or found a substitute source of service as a result of union demands to which it was opposed. Nevertheless, one does not normally expect an alternative source of service to a monopoly. The private sector is unlikely to be able to provide services needed during a public-sector strike. To have such a capability, private-sector firms would have to have made a huge and uneconomical investment in excess capacity. Private security agencies could hardly employ enough extra security personnel to meet a city's demand for security services when the police go on strike. The same problem would preclude private hauling firms or schools from providing the needed services in the event of a strike by sanitation workers or public-school teachers. Nor are the private firms likely to develop the capability after a strike breaks out, knowing that they could be shunted aside as soon as labor peace broke out.

Paradoxically, although public-employee unions often have the potential to disrupt a community, the strike is an economic weapon for management as much or more than it is for the union. In a teacher strike, the average teacher loses about $100 a day. The school board is likely to be paying substitutes much less. The rest of the community, including parents, may be inconvenienced in various ways, but provided state law does not require make-up days, the teachers are apt to be the losers.

One can easily visualize all sorts of variations on these themes. What about a strike by off-track-betting employees? Some individuals in the community would be better off, not losing any money to the state. The latter would lose revenues that presumably would have to be made up from some tax source—the losers? Of course, the employees on strike would lose their wages; whether they would be better off or worse off would depend on the settlement.

A strike by sanitation workers might be a financial bonanza for private waste-disposal firms, a disaster for restaurants and hotels and the tourist trade, and an economic standoff but a period of great inconvenience for citizens generally. A strike by the bridge tenders in New York City resulted in major economic losses to many citizens and firms hurt by the collapse of the city's highway system. Many others were severely inconvenienced, but many hotels made more than usual because visitors could not leave the city.

The calculus of winners and losers in public-sector strikes is too complex for generalizations that make no exceptions or qualifications. Clearly, however, public-sector strikes often can be extremely successful even though there is no economic pressure as such on the employer. What counts is political pressure, and this is a clear-cut advantage for public-sector unions for at least two reasons. First, the greater the inconvenience to citizens generally, the more likely they are to put pressure on the public employer to settle by making concessions to the union. Even when the union's demands are patently unreasonable, the damage being inflicted on many citizens and companies may be so great that they urge a settlement on the union's terms. The businessman who is losing $1000 a day as a result of a strike by public-transit workers realizes that his individual share of the cost of union demands is miniscule, whereas his losses if the strike continues will be substantial. It is difficult to stand on principle in this situation, except perhaps the principle of looking out for oneself.

The other factor that tends to give public employees an extra advantage in strike situations also relates to the political dimension of the problem. A strike usually brings about a situation in which the public employer faces intense pressures to make concessions within a brief period of time. For a variety of reasons, it is usually impractical to develop an informed citizenry before a strike, and it is often impossible to do so during a strike. On the other hand, the union can time its strike and be prepared for maximum political impact when it occurs. It is much more difficult, and usually very expensive, for the public agency to remain prepared for a strike.

For legal and political reasons, the public employer is rarely able to lock out employees. Public-sector unions have been known to meet each morning to decide whether to strike on that day—or even to decide which employees will strike. In some cases, they have succeeded in forcing public employers to employ substitute employees who were not needed when the regular employees showed up for work. Thus the public employer is faced with this dilemma: Either be unprepared for a strike or risk employing replacements who will not be needed if regular employees continue to work. Private-sector employees could take decisive action to forestall this course of conduct, whereas public-sector employers ordinarily cannot. A public employer could not refuse to permit its employees to begin work at 8:00 a.m. because the employees were meeting at 7:00 a.m. to decide whether or not to strike.

The Disadvantages of Public Employment

Thus far, the differences between the public and private sectors seem to favor public employees. Needless to say, there are differences that are disadvantageous to them, both in terms of their overall ability to achieve benefits and in their ability to strike effectively.

The major disadvantage of public employees is that improvements in their benefit level must be achieved through the political process. Normally, the private-sector employer can increase benefits or negotiate an agreement without public or political opposition. For instance, in bargaining, the private employer is bound when its representative signs the agreement. Achieving agreement within a public agency tends to be a more elaborate and more difficult problem. In effect, the difference is between achieving a consensus on a political issue and achieving a management decision on an economic issue. The greater difficulties of achieving a consensus may serve as a brake on what management is willing to do. For example, a city council may be unwilling to face the opposition to higher taxes needed for justified increases in public-employee compensation.

Nevertheless, even on this important issue, public employees have some advantages. The employer's financial situation is fairly well known to the union, as is its room for maneuver. Indeed, public-employee-union representatives are sometimes more knowledgeable than public administrators about the municipal budget.

From the union perspective, the basic problem is this: Public-sector labor relations are characterized by the same conflicts of interest that exist in the private sector. The employees want more; the employer, or at least most of its constituents, want the employees to have less. The employees see themselves caught in a conflict that is to be resolved politically. Resolving the conflict politically means that the employees will lose out regardless of the merits of their case. The reason is that the taxpayers who benefit from paying less for public services far outnumber the employees who stand to gain from the higher levels.[15]

It would be foolish to deny the existence of this conflict of interest between the public employees and the taxpayers or to minimize its importance. Nevertheless, it would be equally foolish to ignore the mitigating factors. One is that elected public officials often find it to be in their interest to provide benefits for public employees in exchange for union political support. Nobody is just a taxpayer and nothing else. Thus although the conflict between taxpayers and public employees is real, it is only one of several considerations for the taxpayer in the voting booth, whereas it is just about the whole ball game for the public employees and public-employee unions. Political leaders therefore can frequently cater to public-employee unions without necessarily losing their votes of citizens who pay taxes. In fact, cooperation or even collusion between political leaders and public-employee unions at the expense of taxpayers is as much a fact of life as is the conflict of interest between taxpayers and public employees. Despite the conflict of interest between taxpayer and public employees, the cards may well be stacked against the taxpayer, not the public employees. No doubt they are stacked in different ways in different communities, but the image of public employees beaten down by a vast horde of taxpayers who vote solely on the basis of their role qua taxpayers has some problems.

In general, the disadvantages as well as the advantages of public employment result from limitations on public management that do not exist in the private sector. In general, relatively little attention is paid to the managerial decision-making process in private-sector bargaining; this is a matter of managerial discretion, not political or administrative structure.[16] Partly for this reason, a public-sector wage policy is inherently a more complex matter than a private-sector one; there are political dimensions to the former that are absent in the latter. Because of this political dimension, public managers have less authority and flexibility than private-sector ones. For example, revenues may be uncertain in both, but the private employer has more flexibility to shift budget allocations to meet wage demands. In other words, because a public-sector wage policy is inherently a governmental decision, every step in the decision-making process is characterized by constraints that do not exist or exist in a much more attenuated form in the private sector. In the aggregate, these constraints constitute a serious disadvantage of public employment.

Another disadvantage of public employees is that their political activities are often limited in ways that do not apply to others. It is difficult to assess the effects of these limitations because they vary widely from state to state. At one extreme, states have prohibited political activity by public employees except for voting and the private expression of the employee's views. A typical statute to this effect reads as follows:

> No employee can be a member of a party, officer of a partisan political club, candidate, or shall take any part in the management or affairs of any political party or in any political campaign, except he may express his opinion, vote and attend meetings to become informed of candidates and issues. [Arizona Rev. Stat., Section 41-772(b).]

The prevalence of such statutes is declining, but many states prohibit political activity during the work day, while the employee is in uniform, or on public facilities. Public employees in some jurisdictions are also required to resign or take a leave of absence if they run for political office. There are also restrictions in some states on the rights of public employees to hold public office or office in a political party concurrently with public employment.[17]

Not surprisingly, the increasing political strength of public-sector unions is weakening the restrictions on public employees. Statutes designed to limit political activity on the job and narrowly drawn so as to protect the First Amendment rights of public employees, appear to be as restrictive as most states will go. Of course, such statutes would not affect full-time union leaders who are not public employees. Such officials may, however, be affected by limitations on the political activities of public-sector unions, as distinguished from public employees individually.

It should be noted that private-sector employers frequently limit employee political activity on the job. For this reason also, the political restrictions on public employees do not appear to be a major comparative disadvantage. As Roumell and Galvin point out, "On the state level, there is clear evidence of a definite movement toward allowing full expression of political freedom by public servants, as long as it is divorced from the employment setting."[18]

Equity: Rationale or Rationalization?

If public-sector employees lack equity because they do not have bargaining rights, the inequity would presumably be manifested in the actual terms and conditions of public employment. Indeed, to ascertain whether there are inequities between the two sectors, it would seem more realistic to compare their actual terms and conditions of employment. The procedural differences in how terms and conditions of employment are established in the two sectors are usually intended to be only an indirect measure of their actual differences in terms and conditions of employment.

Let us rephrase the issue for greater clarity. Other things being equal, the absence of bargaining rights would be an inequity adversely affecting public-sector employees. We have seen, however, that other things are not necessarily equal; it is at least arguable that even in the absence of bargaining rights, public-sector employees enjoy an overall procedural advantage over private-sector employees. Nevertheless, rather than trying to decide which group, if any, is better off *procedurally*, why not compare their actual terms and conditions of employment? The latter comparison should be the more useful, inasmuch as it would provide direct evidence on the issue that is being assessed only indirectly by comparing the procedural differences.

In other words, if public employees are paid more but work less than private-sector employees, the argument that the former suffer a serious inequity because they do not have bargaining rights loses a great deal of its force. By the same token, if public employees are actually paid less but work longer and harder than private-sector employees, the alleged procedural advantages of public employment become suspect. Obviously there are some problems with this approach. For example, certain positions in one sector often have no meaningful counterpart in the other sector, at least in the same geographical area. Police, firefighters, and prison guards are examples of this lack of comparability. Similarly, many private-sector positions are not found in the public sector. However, many positions do have counterparts in both sectors. Secretaries, teachers, accountants, attorneys, custodians, and mechanics are only a few of the positions that are the same or substantially similar in the two sectors.

Ideally, it would be desirable to compare employees in these comparable positions in at least three different ways: (1) wages, (2) fringe benefits, and (3) work loads. The evidence on these issues is neither plentiful, consistent, nor overwhelming. Nevertheless, the preponderance of the evidence supports the conclusion that even without bargaining rights, public employees are better off than private-sector employees with bargaining rights.[19]

Hamermesh analyzed the effects of municipal ownership of transit services on wage rates. He concluded that public ownership resulted in a compensation level 9 to 12 percent above what it would be under private ownership. As he noted, the Amalgated Transit Union was "quite sensible" in supporting "the prompt acquisition of all private transit companies by public bodies."[20]

A study by Perloff compared wage rates of public- and private-sector employees in 11 cities. The study covered both occupations which were and were not generally unionized. Perloff found that in 9 of the 11 cities, the public employees tended to receive higher rates of pay.[21]

Comparative studies such as those just cited do not firmly establish a higher benefit level in public employment. The crucial point, however, is that they clearly do not support the conclusion that public employees are not as well paid or well treated as employees in the private sector; the argument for public-sector bargaining simply cannot sustain the burden of proof on this issue. This inability may help to explain why specific comparisons are rarely used to justify public-sector bargaining.

Reviewing the differences between public and private employment, these possibilities come to mind:

1. Private-sector employees have so many more advantages over public employees that we should enact public-sector bargaining laws and/or legalize strikes by public employees to reduce the gap.
2. Public-sector employees have or can achieve equity with private-sector employees without the right to bargain collectively and to strike.
3. Private-sector bargaining rights for public-sector employees are precisely what is needed to provide equity between public and private-sector employment.

In my opinion, the third option is the least likely. In fact, it is wildly improbable. Given the important differences between the two sectors, the conclusion that private-sector bargaining rights are what is needed to establish equity is clearly a conclusion reached on some nonempirical ground; the conclusion is too neat for the complexity of the data. No one as yet has weighed the differences in a meaningful way and come up with the conclusion that public-sector employees are short of equity with private-sector ones by a margin equal to private-sector rights under the NLRA. Yet as the statement by the NEA's executive director, quoted earlier, illustrates, the public-sector unions are wedded to this highly improbable conclusion.

In assessing the equities, it should be noted that most of the advantages of public employment are ineradicable, regardless of the political jurisdiction involved. Short of disenfranchising public employees, we cannot eliminate their additional leverage on their employer through the political process. Similarly, the rights of public employees to due process are grounded in the federal Constitution, and it is not realistic to anticipate the elimination of these rights through the political process. If therefore equity is to be achieved, it must be achieved by adjusting the representational rather than the constitutional rights of public employees. To compensate for the inherent advantages of public employment, such adjustment should provide representational rights that are different from private-sector bargaining rights. Everyone is entitled to draw his own conclusion about whether public-sector rights to representation and self-help should be more or less than private-sector rights, but we can be most skeptical of those who contend that they ought to be identical.

One final observation. The controversies over public-sector bargaining did not challenge the assumption that equity for public-sector employees is a desirable objective, nor do I intend to argue the issue here. Nevertheless, the assumption is by no means as settled as one might infer from the lack of attention accorded it.

First of all, whether there should be equity between employees in the two sectors is primarily a political, not an economic, issue. Second, regardless of past or present attitudes on the issue, we cannot foreclose the possibility that many communities, or even our society as a whole, might be consciously opposed to equity for public employees. For instance, a community or a state might regard a high level of public-employee benefits as undesirable, or even dangerous, to a free society. Citizens and taxpayers might support increased private control over spending decisions, even if such control requires a lower level of compensation for public employees. Inasmuch as the latter accept employment knowing that it is subject to the political process, they have no inherent permanent right to equity with private-sector employees.

Both supporters and opponents of public-sector bargaining have ignored this issue to date. Nevertheless, it exists, and it constitutes a potential threat to public-sector bargaining. Does the electorate have the political right to maintain the benefits of public employment at a lower level than private-sector benefits? And if it does and if it deliberately exercises this right, the argument that public-sector bargaining is needed to esablish equity for public employees becomes irrelevant. The issue is whether bargaining norms should dominate our political processes or whether our political processes should take precedence over bargaining norms. This issue emerges in many forms throughout this book; in some respects, it is the single most important issue relating to public-sector bargaining.

Notes

1. Terry Herndon, "The Case for Collective Bargaining Statutes," *Phi Delta Kappan* (May 1979):651-652. Reprinted with permission.

2. In California, the *Final Report of the Assembly Advisory Council on Public Employee Relations* relied heavily on this argument in recommending the legalization of strikes by public employees. See the *Final Report*, pp. 199-200. The report as a whole is discussed in chapter 7.

3. *Perry* v. *Sindermann* (1972) 408 U.S. 593.

4. William J. Grimshaw, *Union Rule in the Schools* (Lexington, Mass.: Lexington Books, D.C. Heath, 1979).

5. For a convincing statement of this position, see William E. Simon, *A Time for Truth* (New York: Berkley Publishing, 1978), chapter 5.

6. *AFSME in the Public Service*, Q.A. L-136 (Washington, D.C.: American Federation of State, County, and Municipal Employees, AFL-CIO, n.d.).

7. The interested reader will find examples of this legislation in Sections 45100 to 45423 of California's Reorganized Education Code, operative 30 April 1977.

8. See Lawyers Committee for Civil Rights Under Law, *State Legal Standards for the Provision of Public Education: An Overview* (Washington, D.C.: National Institute of Education, U.S. Department of Health, Education and Welfare, November 1978); and Myron Lieberman, *Identification and Evaluation of Legal Constraints on Educational Productivity*, Project No. 3-0231 (Washington, D.C.: National Institute of Education, U.S. Department of Health, Education and Welfare, 1 June 1975), pp. 26-76.

9. For a discussion of this issue, see Arvid Anderson and Joan Weitzman, "The Scope of Bargaining in the Public Sector," in Public Employment Relations Services, *Portrait of a Process: Collective Bargaining in Public Employment* (Ft. Washington, Penn.: Labor Relations Press, 1979), pp. 173-195. See also Joyce M. Najita, "The Scope of Negotiations," *Guide to Statutory Provisions in Public Sector Bargaining*, 2nd issue (Hawaii: Industrial Relations Center, University of Hawaii, July 1978).

10. For interindustry differences in extent of unionization, see U.S. Department of Labor, Bureau of Labor Statistics, *Directory of National Unions and Employee Associations* (Washington, D.C.: Government Printing Office, 1979), pp. 70-73.

11. *NLRB* v. *IBEW, Local 1229*, 346 U.S. 464 (1953).

12. *Patterson Sargent Co.* v. *NLRB* 1627 (1956), 316.

13. For an excellent discussion of the loyalty issue in the private sector, see Robert A. Gorman, *Basic Text on Labor Law, Unionization and Collective Bargaining* (St. Paul, Minn.: West Publishing, 1976), pp. 314-317.

14. See *Pickering* v. *Board of Education* 391 U.S. 563 (1968).

15. Perhaps the most cogent analysis of the inherent disadvantages facing public employees is found in Clyde W. Summers, "Public Employee Bargaining: A Political Perspective," *Yale Law Journal* 83 (1974):1156-1200. Summers concluded that the disadvantages justified public-sector bargaining. Unfortunately, he did not examine or even recognize the inherent advantages as well as the disadvantages of public employment, at least in this article.

16. See Clyde W. Summers, "Public Employee Bargaining," and "Public Sector Bargaining: Problems of Governmental Decisionmaking," *University of Cincinnati Law Review* 44 (1975):669-679.

17. A good summary may be found in George T. Roumell, Jr., and Thomas J. Galvin, "Protection of the Integrity of Each Party from Domination by the Other," in Public Employment Relations Services, *Portrait of a Process*, pp. 327-360. See also Harry Edwards, R. Theodore Clark, Jr., and Charles B. Craver, *Labor Relations Law in the Public Sector*, 2nd ed. (Indianapolis: Bobbs-Merrill, 1979), pp. 743-779.

18. Roumell and Galvin, "Protection of the Integrity," p. 352.

19. Daniel S. Hamermesh, ed., *Labor in the Public and Nonprofit Sectors* (Princeton, N.J.: Princeton University Press, 1975); and Harry T. Edwards, R. Theodore Clark, Jr., and Charles B. Craver, *Labor Relations Law in the Public Sector*, 2nd ed. (Indianapolis: Bobbs-Merrill, 1979), p. 79.

20. Hamermesh, *Labor in the Public and Nonprofit Sectors*, p. 238.

21. S. Perloff, "Comparing Municipal, Industry and Federal Pay," *Monthly Labor Review* 94 (October 1971):46-50.

4 The Political Nature of Public-Sector Bargaining

The primary issue discussed in this chapter is whether public-sector bargaining can be reconciled with the fundamental elements of democratic representative government. What are these elements? The following list suggested by Summers (using school boards as an example) would probably be widely accepted.

(1) only duly elected officials could vote
(2) issues to be voted on would be defined (with or without discussion) by administrators, board members, or some member of the public
(3) the public would often (though not always) have advance notice of at least important issues to be voted on
(4) there would usually be considerable opportunity for interested members of the public and for board members to gather information and hear opinions prior to voting
(5) as to important matters, some form of parliamentary procedure would be followed with its provisions for amendment of and deliberation on proposals
(6) at least on important issues, there would usually be opportunity for opponents and proponents to use publicity, media, and other means to rally public support
(7) final votes by board members would be taken, with the principle of majority rule controlling
(8) resulting rules and policy would be embodied in minutes, board rules and regulations, policy statements or the like.[1]

The argument that public-sector bargaining is not consistent with some or all of these elements of the democratic process is most visible and easily understood in strike situations. For this reason, it shall be discussed in that context first. Subsequently, it can be more readily understood whether the argument applies to situations in which strikes are not a factor.

As pointed out in chapter 3, labor-relations experts disagree over whether there can be collective bargaining without the right to strike. Whichever view is correct, the American labor movement has avoided using strikes as political weapons. Collective bargaining and strikes have been viewed as means of achieving economic benefits for organized employees. Unlike the situation in many other countries, strikes have not been used in the United States for political objectives. In this sense at least, the labor movement in the United States has been a conservative one.

Public-sector strikes constitute a basic rupture of this tradition. To public employees, "terms and conditions of employment" in the public sector seem to be essentially similar to their counterpart in the private sector. Nevertheless, there is a crucial difference. The terms and conditions of employment for public employees are public policies, whatever else they are or appear to be. As the Supreme Court has noted, "Finally, decisionmaking by a public employer is above all a political process. . . ."[2] In the same case, Justice Powell observed that,

> The ultimate objective of a union in the public sector, like that of a political party, is to influence public decisionmaking in accordance with the views and perceived interests of its membership. . . . The union's objective is to obtain favorable decisions—and to place persons in positions of power who will be receptive to the union's viewpoint.
>
> What distinguishes the public sector union from the political party—and the distinction is a limited one—is that most of its members are employees who share similar economic interests and who *may* have a common professional perspective on some issues of public policy. . . .

The logical implication of these quotations (and countless others to the same effect) is that a strike over terms and conditions of public employment is inherently an effort to modify public policy by the collective withdrawal of public services.[3]

Under what conditions, if any, should the collective withdrawal of a public service by public employees be a legally acceptable political tactic? This is a crucial issue in state and local public employment today.

Essentially, the argument against legalization is that public-sector strikes cannot be reconciled with the democratic process. The reason is that under strike conditions, nonemployee organizations and individuals are unfairly and undemocratically excluded from the process of establishing public policy.

As an example, consider teacher proposals concerning hours of employment. Such proposals include the number and scheduling of teacher work days and number and scheduling of evening meetings (such as Back-to-School Night), and the extent of adjunct duties such as parent conferences. Whatever policies are ultimately adopted by school boards on these issues are public policies, just as speed limits or parking regulations or income taxes are public policies. Parents, students, farmers, businessmen, other school-district employees, and many other groups have a legitimate interest in how many days teachers work, when the schoolyear begins and when it ends, the number and frequency of evening meetings, teacher availability for parent conferences, and so on. These groups can react to proposals by the school board or teacher union that are public knowledge for a reasonable time. It is, however, practically impossible for them to react effectively to proposals made days or even just a few hours before a strike deadline. Indeed, if they learn of such proposals at all, they normally do so when the complete agreement is made public—at which time the last-minute proposals are a fait accompli, from the standpoint of everyone except the union. Nevertheless, last-minute agreements, often hammered out in round-the-clock bargaining just before a strike deadline, are typically the way public agencies avoid a strike.

The strike situation only highlights a problem that characterizes public-sector bargaining generally. Under bargaining, public officials negotiate public policies with the one interest group that has the most to gain from its exclusive access to policymakers. The policies that emerge frequently have adverse long-range consequences to others that are not and cannot be assessed properly until others know what they are, have a genuine opportunity to study them, and can give their views before the public agency becomes irrevocably committed to them. As a matter of fact, the practice of negotiating public policies with special-interest groups and then legislating them before others concerned have an opportunity to study and react is usually a matter for indignant criticism.

Ratification and the Bargaining-Political Dilemma

In the private sector, the employer sends a representative to bargain. When this representative agrees, the employer is bound. The relationship between the employer and the employer's chief negotiator are not important public-policy considerations, provided that the negotiator has the authority to negotiate on behalf of the employer.

As Summers has lucidly pointed out, public-sector bargaining presents an altogether different situation.[4] The negotiators are negotiating public, that is, governmental policies. The negotiator for the public agency may be unable to make a commitment because the agency depends on some other source such as state aid for its revenues. Similarly, the negotiator may be affected by a state requirement that limits contracts to one year or that prescribes notice procedures before local governments can adopt public policies. Of course, procedures governing the establishment of public policy can and do change. The crucial issue, however, is whether public-sector bargaining eliminates or greatly erodes the safeguards and limitations placed on governmental decision making by the democratic process.

That an issue exists is evident if we compare the procedures for approving the policies in a labor agreement with the procedures for approving other public policies. With respect to the latter, a public official can change his mind any time prior to ratification without incurring any legal risks or sanctions. Changing one's mind overnight on a housing ordinance may be costly politically, but such change is not prohibited legally in any way. Under public-sector bargaining, however, public officials become legally as well as practically committed to support public policies before the community as a whole has had an opportunity to know about, let alone consider, them. The reason is that the public employer risks a sustainable unfair-labor-practice charge for its refusal to ratify a tentative agreement negotiated by its representatives. This point is so important that some elaboration of it is essential.

First, we must recognize that the individuals who negotiate a labor agreement are legally bound to support its ratification. This is true in both the public and private sectors. It is ordinarily an unfair labor practice for a party to oppose an agreement which that party has negotiated at the table. The practical significance of this fact in the public sector relates to the identity of the negotiators for the public employer. If the negotiators are individuals who must ratify the agreement, they have lost the effective right to refuse to ratify. As to them at least, citizen reaction to a tentative agreement would be irrelevant; it would be an unfair labor practice, subject to legal remedies, for such individuals to oppose approval of the agreement they had negotiated.

For example, suppose a mayor heads up the municipal bargaining team. Agreement is reached with the municipal unions on a new contract. If the mayor changes his mind and votes against ratification, the municipality would ordinarily be guilty of an unfair labor practice, and be subject to the remedies ordered by the state PERB.

One obvious implication is that public agencies should avoid having any individual who must ratify also serving on the agency's negotiating team. This can be a difficult problem, for example in small school districts; except for the superintendent, board members may constitute the pool from which the negotiating team must be chosen. The issue could arise, however, even in the largest jurisdictions where elected officals are not regular members of the bargaining team. When, however, bargaining reaches a crisis point, the top elected officials who must ratify the agreement often join the management bargaining team, in order to make the crucial decisions on a contract. A mayor might do this, and discover the next morning that some crucial considerations had been overlooked in reaching an agreement. Unfortunately, the mayor who tried to renege on the agreement for this reason would be just as guilty of an unfair labor practice as a private-sector negotiator who had second thoughts about an agreement he had reached.

Let us now consider the implication of this fact for citizen participation. The agreement at the table having been tentative, it is usually necessary for the public employer to ratify it. Consequently, ratification of the agreement (that is, adoption of various public policies) is placed on the agenda of the public employer. Citizens are accorded the right to speak to the desirability of these policies. However, insofar as they are speaking to individuals who negotiated the agreement, they are speaking to the stone deaf.

As a matter of fact, some states have statutorily dispensed with the requirement that the public employer conduct a hearing and/or formally adopt the policies negotiated with the union. The negotiated policies do not *become* public policies; they *are* public policies when agreed upon during negotiations. Thus Section 201.12 of New York's Taylor Law defines an agreement as

> the result of the exchange of mutual promises between the chief executive officer of a public employer and an employee organization which becomes a binding contract, for the period set forth therein, except as to any provisions therein which require approval by a legislative body, and as to those provisions, shall become binding when the appropriate legislative body gives its approval.

In an unfair-labor-practice case decided in 1973, the New York PERB asserted,

> In this connection, we note that CSL §201.12 defines an agreement as an exchange of mutual promises between the school superintendent and the employee organization. The statutory role of the Board of Education is limited to the approval of matters that inherently require legislative approval, such as the provision of additional funds. By reserving to itself the right to ratify agreements, the Board of Education interfered with the statutory process of negotiations.[5]

It is hardly debatable that such a provision virtually eliminates third-party participation in the public policymaking process. Although most states have not gone this far, there would probably be unanimous agreement that a negotiator who is also a potential ratifier cannot refuse to support the negotiated agreement. What about a refusal to ratify by public officials who were not negotiators? Clearly, even where ratification is necessary to effectuate a negotiated agreement, and the ratifying authorities were not the negotiators, their right not to ratify is severely limited. Just how limited would be up to each state PERB and would therefore vary from state to state. Clearly, fraud or a good-faith misunderstanding as to the substance of what had been agreed to would be legitimate grounds for refusal to ratify, without subjecting the employer to a sustainable unfair-labor-practice charge. On the other hand, refusal to ratify because of tardy recognition of the consequences of an agreement that was clearly understood could well be an unfair practice. Significantly, prior to the time personnel policies were negotiated, the public authorities ultimately responsible to the electorate for approving them could change their minds about them for any reason up to the last second and suffer no adverse legal consequences as a result of such changes. Such flexibility for policymaking bodies is still the rule, outside the labor-relations area.

An example may help clarify the differences between the public-policy process under public-sector bargaining and the normal democratic process. Suppose a city council wants to enact a housing ordinance. City officials may, and are likely to, meet privately with the interest groups involved—all of them. Let us assume, however, that they meet with only the builders. During the meeting, city officials and builders reach tentative agreement on a new housing ordinance, which is submitted to the city council for ratification.

Even if the city council members had met privately with only the builders—which would be unusual and render the proposed ordinance suspect—the council could change it completely at the public hearing or as a result of the public hearing without being subject to any penalties for doing so. It would not be committing an unfair building practice for reneging on a tentative agreement with a particular interest group. On the contrary, the fact that it had conducted private meetings and reached agreement with only one interest group would be deemed all the more reason for giving good-faith consideration to other views and making changes before adoption of a housing ordinance. Furthermore, if the builders objected to a proposed ordinance, they would have no legal right to force the city council to respond to every builder's proposal, no right to force the city council to enter into mediation and fact-finding on their differences with the council, and no right to preclude any change in the existing housing ordinance until all these impasse procedures had been exhausted.

It is frequently asserted that unions have refused to ratify negotiated agreements and have not been subject to unfair-practice charges for such refusals. Therefore, it is often thought that the public employer can do so likewise.

This contention errs in at least two ways. First, the unions are not legally free to refuse to ratify a negotiated agreement for any reason whatsoever. A recent Oregon case makes this clear. The union refused to ratify because it wanted to add a "fair share," that is an agency-shop clause to the tentative agreement. The public employer showed that a mutually agreed upon deadline for submitting new proposals had passed by the time the union made its proposal. Under these circumstances, the Oregon PERB held the union to be guilty of an unfair labor practice and ordered it to ratify the tentative agreement.[6] It is seldom as useful to the employer as it is to the union to press unfair-labor-practice charges over a refusal to ratify, but this does not vitiate the fact that both parties have lost some freedom at the point of a tentative agreement.

The legal changes in the governmental decision-making process required by public-sector bargaining are not the only reasons why such bargaining inhibits third-party participation in the process. The dynamics of bargaining suggest another reason why citizen comment on a proposed contract would be virtually always futile. During bargaining, negotiators for public employers communicate frequently with their principals (mayor, school board, and so on). One purpose of such communications is to inform the decision-making officials about union proposals and reactions. Another purpose is to elicit decisions or guidelines on what concessions can be made to the union in bargaining. As most experienced negotiators know, the only mistake worse than surprising the other party is to surprise your own at the climax of negotiations. For this reason, the public employer is psychologically and strategically as well as legally committed to the entire agreement as it finally emerges at the table. At that point, the public employer is most definitely not looking for informed criticisms and suggestions from third parties to improve the policies about to be adopted as part of the contract. On the contrary, the public employer's attitude is to have the agreement ratified as quickly as possible so that nobody on either side upsets this carefully balanced applecart. Thus in bargaining, one of the most common scenarios is for the parties to reach agreement after prolonged negotiations just before some deadline, the employees meet immediately to ratify the contract, and the body that ratifies for the public agency meets that same evening, or as soon as is legally possible, pursuant to a special meeting if necessary, in order to "wrap things up."

Note that the objection to public-sector bargaining does not consist of the fact that public and union representatives meet behind closed doors or that they reach tentative agreements during such meetings. It lies primarily in the fact that such tentative agreements become legally binding on the public agency before the public has had a chance to consider them and to express views that justify changes in them; by the time of the formal ratification vote, if there is one, third parties have lost the effective right to modify the agreement, even though they were excluded from the process that led to its adoption. Unlike a hearing on a housing ordinance, a hearing on a public-sector labor agreement is of no value to others; the public employer is already locked into the agreement. The differences between the bargaining-law states on this issue are not as important as the fact that all of them significantly circumscribe the freedom of policymaking bodies (city council, school boards, boards of supervisors, and so on) to adopt whatever policies they wish regardless of when their desirability became evident.

As might be expected, public-sector unions have a position on this issue. According to this position, third parties are part of the public represented by the public employer's negotiating team. Therefore, it is the responsibility of the public employer to ascertain the view of others and take them into account in the negotiations. This position is clearly untenable. When proposals and counterproposals are made in the climatic stages of bargaining, it is practically impossible to inform the community about them and elicit informed reactions to them. Even if it were possible to predict well in advance the substance of the proposals to be laid on the table at the terminal stages of bargaining (and it is frequently, if not usually, not possible), the bargainist position would be untenable. The acceptability of many proposals not only to the public employer but to third parties often depends on how they relate to a total package. A given salary proposal may be acceptable to taxpayers in one package, unacceptable in others. Legally speaking, the public employer does represent third parties in bargaining; practically speaking, however, such representation is ineffective or impossible if the public employer cannot consult with third parties because of a lack of time or because such consultation must take place at times and places (such as the early morning hours before a strike deadline), that preclude it. The inescapable reality is that public-sector bargaining is a bilateral, not a multilateral, process.

Political or Bargaining Norms as Governing the Ratification of Public-Sector Labor Agreements

In retrospect, the conflict between political and bargaining norms in public-sector bargaining seems obvious. Be that as it may, the conflict was not articulated in professional literature until 1969 and then primarily in media such as law-review journals, which did not enjoy a large audience. By this time, public-sector bargaining had achieved irreversible political momentum, and the caveats concerning its impact on governmental decision making were simply brushed aside or ignored altogether.

Is it possible or feasible to have public-sector bargaining but to restore political supremacy over the ratification process, that is, over the adoption of public personnel policies? One suggestion is to submit public-sector labor agreements to a referendum. In all likelihood, however, sheer mechanical problems of doing so render this solution impractical. Providing the electorate with a complete agreement would be prohibitively expensive; providing it with less would raise difficult questions of condensation and voter confusion over the substance. More importantly, there would normally be a considerable lag between tentative agreement and a referendum. The nature of the interim policies would be only one problem; another might be the nature of the policies to be followed when contracts were voted down. And in jurisdictions that had to bargain with several unions, the referendum would be a year-round process.

In a uncharacteristic burst of irrationality, Wellington and Winter suggest a referendum on specific items, subject to voter petition within a fixed period of time after an agreement is negotiated.[7] Such a possibility would enormously complicate bargaining; union representatives would be preoccupied with the dangers of making concessions in exchange for benefits that might be nullified by referenda. Were this suggestion adopted, public-sector agreements could hardly include the standard separability provision, that is, that the remainder of an agreement is still valid even if any provision of it is invalid as a matter of law. Even Wellington and Winter were concerned that their suggestion would undermine bargaining. This would happen if it were relatively easy to initiate a referendum. On the other hand, if it were difficult to do so, the requirements of democratic political process would not be met with respect to the negotiated policies.

To this observer, it appears that direct voter referenda on negotiated agreements, or provisions thereof, is not an especially promising approach. It may be useful as a safeguard against extreme positions by either public employers or public-employee unions, but even this is far from clear. Later in this chapter, however, it is suggested that negotiating schedules be coordinated with election schedules, instead of budgetary deadlines. This would make possible a timely vote on the public officials responsible for negotiating agreements; presumably, these officials would have to be responsive to the community, knowing that the agreements they had negotiated could become a political issue within a month or two.

Suppose there were negotiations but the employer could change the tentative agreement prior to formal ratification without being subject to unfair-labor-practice charges. What would be the effects of such a change on the bargaining itself? And to what extent would third parties become active in efforts to modify tentative agreements?

Needless to say, public-sector unions would resist any such change to the utmost. They would assert, and perhaps rightly so, that such a possibility would destroy bargaining. In any case, the possibility is envisaged here primarily as a response to a judicial attack on public-sector bargaining or as a legislative outcome in a state with only marginal support for public-sector bargaining.

Prebargaining experience suggests that there might be little intervention by third parties. Such intervention was minimal prior to the advent of bargaining. There might well be even less after bargaining since public employers are more likely to be committed to a negotiated agreement. On the other hand, the low level of involvement by third parties in the prebargaining era may be misleading. The potential for such involvement undoubtedly affected the policies adopted so as to make actual involvement unnecessary.

Nevertheless, the legal possibility that the public employer could change a negotiated agreement would probably have a major effect on the bargaining. Public-sector unions would be less likely to resist employer demands to the point of impasse if they knew that the employer could adopt its proposal within a short time, regardless of union opposition. It would be better for the union to get concessions in exchange for such employer demands than to have them adopted unilaterally, without any concessions to the union. Of course, several variations are possible. It would be possible to limit the time in which the employer could act unilaterally or to spell out statutorily acceptable and nonacceptable bases for modification. To this extent, the limitations on the employer's freedom would still be inconsistent with our normal political processes, but complete consistency may not be attainable.

Of course, the possibility that third parties would not intervene anyway at the point of ratification cannot be a union argument for prohibiting such intervention. It hardly makes sense to urge a drastic change in our political process if such change is unlikely to have any practical effect. Why exclude third parties and prohibit a public employer from unilaterally changing a tentative agreement after public reaction to it if in practice such changes would rarely be necessary? The more it is contended that third parties do not care about public-sector labor agreements, the less justification there is for denying public employers complete legal freedom to change tentative agreements unilaterally prior to their ratification or for adopting drastic changes in our political processes to accommodate public-sector bargaining. The inescapable reality, however, is that collective bargaining is essentially a bilateral process, whereas public policymaking has always been deemed to be a multilateral process, accessible to all on equal terms.

Sunshine Bargaining and the Policymaking Process

In most states, it would be an unfair labor practice for either party to insist that bargaining sessions be open to third parties, that is, to outsiders. Wherever this issue has been raised, the PERBs have ruled that insistence on the public's right to attend bargaining sessions is an unfair labor practice. In contrast, six states (Florida, Kansas, Minnesota, Oklahoma, Tennessee, and Texas) have adopted a form of "sunshine bargaining" as a means of reconciling public-sector bargaining with the basic elements of the democratic policymaking process.[8] Under sunshine bargaining, public-sector bargaining must be open to the public. Theoretically, this means that individuals or representatives of other groups can be present at all bargaining sessions.

Despite its supporters and the fact that it may have salutary effects in some situations, sunshine bargaining does not and cannot resolve the inconsistencies between the political process and the bilateral process of collective bargaining. Prefatorily, it should be noted that sunshine laws are easily evaded, especially by employers and unions who wish to do so jointly; however, the following discussion ignores this consideration. In the first place, third parties have no control over the scheduling of bargaining sessions; public employers and public-employee unions can schedule bargaining sessions on short notice at times and places that render attendance by others a practical impossibility.

Furthermore, sunshine laws permit third parties only to attend and observe bargaining. They do not permit others to participate in the bargaining process itself. The result is that other parties do not even attend, at least on a regular or continuing basis. It is difficult to see how it could be otherwise.

Like most legislation on public-sector bargaining, sunshine laws ignore the dynamics of bargaining. For example, a PTA representative will not be able to convene the PTA Executive Committee at 4:00 a.m. to get its reactions to a union proposal made at 3:00 a.m. to avert a strike set for 8:00 a.m. Third parties have no right to participate in the negotiations, no time to confer with their principals, and no right to schedule meetings to present their views. The third parties can listen; and since that is all they can do under sunshine laws, they seldom even do that.

Even in the absence of strikes or strike threats, the dynamics of bargaining render agreement unlikely much before a deadline such as the expiration of the existing agreement. Both sides are reluctant to make concessions early and both tend to hold back until the end of the process. Typically, just before a deadline of some sort, the parties will be busily engaged in negotiating public policies. A tremendous amount of swapping and amending and deleting takes place in the final days, often even the final hours or final minutes of the process. Frequently, negotiations drag on for several months and then move quickly to a settlement as a deadline approaches.

In those last few days or hours, it is practically impossible for anyone except the union and the employer to keep abreast of developments. In thousands of cases, the parties become involved in round-the-clock bargaining in an effort to achieve an agreement by a deadline set by one or both parties or by law. The tendency for issues to be resolved in last-minute negotiations is inherent in the bargaining process. Admittedly, to some extent, it is unavoidable in the legislative process also, but bargaining constitutes a quantum, self-inflicted, and hence gratuitous requirement that public policy be adopted in this way. Under most legislative deadlines such as a requirement that a legislature adjourn by a certain time, interest groups are competing primarily for legislative attention to their cause. In this situation, the problem is not that interest groups are excluded by law from the policymaking process. It is that time is not an infinite resource for legislatures—a "law" that is neither made by legislatures nor is inherently unfair to any particular group.

On the other hand, a sunshine law that met the preceding objections would undermine the bargaining law. Merely permitting third parties to be present at negotiating sessions raises difficult problems of accountability. Suppose the third parties, in an effort to win elective office, or through incompetence, misrepresent what is happening at the bargaining table. Such misrepresentations could easily undermine good-faith bargaining. And if third parties have the right to do anything except listen, what assurance is there—could there be?—that such rights would not be exercised in a harmful way, for purposes unrelated to bargaining? The third parties are not subject to unfair-labor-practice charges or to any other legal controls that would protect the integrity of the bargaining process. Certainly, it would be extreme naiveté to assume that attendees would be reporters knowledgeable about public-sector labor relations (a null category, in this observer's experience) or public-spirited citizens interested primarily in the welfare of the community.

Of course, in the political arena there are no restrictions on citizens analogous to unfair labor practices. Citizens can be as informed or uninformed as they wish. They can show up for every meeting of the city council or some, one, or none. They can be as prepared or as unprepared as they wish, and express the most blatant falsehoods about what did or did not happen at meetings of public agencies.

On this rationale, supporters of sunshine bargaining might argue there is no need or justification for restrictions on third parties at bargaining sessions. Inasmuch as such sessions are devoted to adopting public policy, citizens should have the freedoms associated with political activity. The problem is that if we structure the bargaining process to include third parties with all their political freedoms, we undermine bargaining; if we structure public-sector bargaining to exclude third parties, we undermine our political processes.

This issue arises in many ways in addition to third-party access to negotiating sessions. For example, most of the state bargaining laws provide for fact finding at some stage of the impasse procedure. The issue arises: At what stage should the recommendations of the fact-finder be made public? In 1972 New York Governor Nelson Rockefeller asked the New York PERB to submit recommendations on the general problem of disclosure of the status of negotiations. After conducting an extensive survey among negotiators, the media, and the impartial third-party industry, the PERB recommended no changes in the Taylor law, which required only that the PERB release the fact-finder's report no later than five days after having been submitted to the parties.

In explaining its recommendation, the New York PERB posed the issue with unusual clarity:

> Negotiations under the Taylor Law are, in theory at least, between the Chief Executive and the employee organization on behalf of the public and as the public's agent. The Chief Executive is authorized to pursue his policies, and by entering into the contracts to obligate the government to carry out those policies. If disclosure of an agreement of the Chief

Executive is not designed to induce renunciation or modification of that agreement, it is meaningless, adding nothing but costs and delay to ordinary disclosure requirements. If disclosure contemplates renunciation or modification of the agreement, it subverts the authority of the Chief Executive and imperils the negotiation process.[9]

In recommending against disclosure, the New York PERB was clearly subordinating political democracy to public-sector bargaining. In what other policy arena would the public be kept uninformed as a matter of policy so that it could not renounce or amend a policy before it was adopted? If the city fathers were meeting with contractors over housing laws, should the community be kept uninformed until after the policy is officially adopted since to inform it invites "renunciation or modification of the agreement"?

The suggestion to avoid disclosure for this reason is preposterous as is the suggestion that the democratic process is adequately served because the community can vote out of office those who negotiate the agreements involved. The responsible officials may not care about running for the same office again. They may be retiring or planning to run for higher office or quite willing to ride out the storm for any number of reasons. The possibility of voting them out of office from one to four years hence may be of little practical value to others seriously and unfairly disadvantaged by an agreement that binds a public agency before those affected have had an opportunity to react to it. And what about the argument for public-sector bargaining—that it is necessary to provide public employees with an opportunity to react in timely fashion to proposed policies that affect them? To urge that the public be presented with a fait accompli while attempting to salvage the democratic process by a right to vote the negotiating officials out of office hardly rises above the level of apologetics for public-sector bargaining.

Collective Bargaining as Only a Procedural Requirement

A crucial argument made to support public-sector bargaining is that it does not curtail the rights of public employers to adopt whatever substantive policies they wish. According to this argument, public-sector bargaining is merely a procedural requirement without substantive policy implications. Duly elected officials still retain their decision-making powers and establish public policies. Collective bargaining merely ensures that elected officials consider the views of public employees before exercising their rights to act on matters affecting such employees.

Perhaps an analogy will help clarify this crucial argument. For decades, public-employee organizations have supported tenure laws. As we have seen, they have been very successful in enacting such laws; for example, more than 40 states have a teacher-tenure law. Theoretically, such laws do not prohibit public employers from firing incompetent public employees. Instead, they prescribe the procedures to be followed in order to effectuate the firing. The procedures are intended to ensure that public employees are fired only for good cause. They are not intended to protect incompetent employees from dismissal. Conceptually, they are supposed to provide fair treatment for employees without impinging on the basic prerogatives of public employers.

The tenure laws vary widely from state to state. In some states they require only advance notice, a written statement of the reason, and an opportunity to rebut the reasons. In other states, however, the tenure laws prescribe detailed, complex, and costly procedures in which even a technical violation may prove fatal to management's rights to fire a public employee. In such states, management often does not even try to fire incompetent employees; the procedural requirements render it futile to do so.

It is not necessary here to attempt to decide what is fair procedure in these matters. All that is necessary is to recognize that procedural requirements could become so onerous that they would unreasonably inhibit a public employer from taking an action in the public interest. Similar issues arise in many other fields; for example, it is often alleged that the procedural requirements placed on law-enforcement agencies unreasonably forces them to drop charges against individuals clearly guilty of criminal conduct. Manufacturers and developers frequently complain that environmental-protection laws impose such unreasonable and costly procedural requirements that they cannot function. Again it is unnecessary to pass on the merits of specific claims. The point is that procedural requirements can vary tremendously, and can, theoretically at least, impose unreasonable obligations on individuals or agencies subject to them.

With this caveat in mind, let us consider the argument that public-sector bargaining is "only" or "merely" a procedural requirement that does not prevent public employers from adopting whatever personnel policies they wish. In this case, the procedural requirement is allegedly intended only to ensure that public employees get an adequate opportunity to express their views and that the public employer make a good-faith effort to reach agreement with the employees before making a final decision on personnel policies.

This argument is based on the law, both in the private sector and in the bargaining-law states. For example, under the NLRA, the duty to bargain "does not compel either party to agree to a proposal or require the making of a concession" (*Section* 8,d, NLRA). The employer's legal obligation is only to bargain in good faith. Having fulfilled that obligation, the employer is free to act unilaterally if there is no agreement. The vast majority of state laws include language similar or identical to the language of the NLRA on this issue. The major exceptions appear to be the laws (to be discussed in the next chapter) that require public employers and public-sector unions to submit their interest disputes to some form of binding arbitration. Such laws usually apply only to police and/or firefighters; regardless, the following discussion does not necessarily apply to situations covered by such laws.

Whether or not public-sector bargaining per se is only procedural, the actual state bargaining statutes are not always limited to procedural matters. As table 4-1 shows, such statutes frequently mandate or prohibit substantive personnel policies.

Obviously, by getting the bargaining statute to include the item, the union (or management, if a concession to management is involved) precludes the necessity of having to negotiate for it on an employer-by-employer basis. Not only is statewide success on the item assured but no concessions need be made at the local level to achieve it. The crucial point here, however, is that one must look to the actual statutes, not to the arguments for public-sector bargaining, to ascertain whether any substantive provisions are included or excluded, that is, to ascertain whether the statute is only procedural on its face.

Let us now turn to the procedural issue itself. Is it correct to say that public employers retain the right to adopt whatever policies they wish, subject only to the procedural requirement that they consider the views of employee representatives, and make a good-faith effort to reach agreement on matters subject to negotiation? To assess this argument, it is necessary to review some legal principles of collective bargaining. One is that the employer may not act unilaterally after the expiration of a contract until it has fulfilled its obligation to bargain in good faith. In the public sector, this obligation is usually considered to have been met legally when the impasse procedures have been completed. The period of time required to complete

Table 4-1
Personnel Policies Mandated or Prohibited by State Public-Employee-Bargaining Statutes

Number of States	Policy Mandated or Prohibited
25	Public employer must provide dues deduction
18	Management-rights clause in bargaining statute
15	Limits on duration of contracts
7	Require grievance arbitration in the contract
6	Agency shop prohibited
6	Union shop prohibited
5	Agency shop mandated
2	Grievance arbitration prohibited

Source: Labor-Management Services Administration, Summary of Public Sector Labor Relations Policies (Washington, D.C.: U.S. Department of Labor, 1979), p. 65.

the impasse procedures varies from state to state and situation to situation, but it frequently requires several months. In states where fact-finding is a part of the procedure, it often takes three to six months or longer to complete the impasse procedures.

During this time the public employer may not act unilaterally on the matters subject to bargaining—leaves, transfers, wages, hours, assignment, and so on. Although the contract has expired, the provisions in it constitute the status quo that the employer may not change until it has fulfilled its obligation to bargain. With a few exceptions that do not change the basic point, the union exercises an effective legal veto power over employer action after the expiration of a contract; during the contract, of course, the employer can act only as it has agreed with the union. As a matter of fact, New York statutorily prohibits public employers from taking unilateral action during negotiations or within 30 days after the report of an impasse panel:

> d. Preservation of status quo. During the period of negotiations between a public employer and a public employee organization concerning a collective bargaining agreement, and, if an impasse panel is appointed during the period commencing on the date on which such panel is appointed and ending thirty days after it submits its report, the public employee organization party to the negotiations, and the public employees it represents, shall not induce or engage in any strikes, slowdowns, work stoppages, or mass absenteeism, nor shall such public employee organization induce any mass resignations, and the public employer shall refrain from unilateral changes in wages, hours, or working conditions. This subdivision shall not be construed to limit the rights of public employers other than their right to make such unilateral changes, or the rights and duties of public employees and employee organizations under state law. For the purpose of this subdivision their term 'period of negotiations' shall mean the period commencing on the date on which a bargaining notice is filed and ending on the date on which a collective bargaining agreement is concluded or an impasse panel is appointed. (NYCCBL §1173-7.0d)

Even in the absence of specific statutory language on the issue, most other states have achieved a similar result by decisions of the state PERBs. In some instances, the public employer even loses the right to act unilaterally upon nonmandatory subjects of bargaining during negotiations or prior to the end of the impasse procedures. This happens if nonmandatory subjects of bargaining were included in a contract being renegotiated or if nonmandatory subjects of bargaining are deemed to have a significant impact on a mandatory one. Along these lines, "PERB's have held that although layoffs are outside the scope of bargaining, the public employer may not layoff employees before bargaining on the 'impact' of layoffs upon mandatory subjects of bargaining, such as severance pay."[10]

What then does it mean to say that "only duly elected officials can vote" on officially adopted public policies? Normally, only the city council can establish traffic regulations. Suppose the law provided that the council could not change these regulations for six months without the approval of *X*—a private citizen or private organization not elected by or responsible to the electorate in any way. Would it still make sense to say that only the city council (that is, duly elected officials) can vote on public policies? Or would it make more sense to say that the power to veto a change in policy is itself the power to make policy? Minimally, unions have the power to ensure that a particular policy or set of policies, even those in an expired collective-bargaining agreement, shall prevail for a significant period of time.

The realities of veto power should not be overlooked. Where elected officials have a veto power over proposed legislation, they are almost always able to extract concessions in exchange for not exercising that power. When that happens, nobody questions the fact that the authority of the legislative body has been shared with the individual with the veto power. The latter's name does not appear on the legislative roll call and may in fact never appear anywhere on the legislation when enacted; regardless, officials with veto power share legislative authority, as distinguished from merely having the ability to influence its exercise.

Essentially, the public-sector union is in the same position as the elected official with the veto power over public policy. The differences are that the union is not elected by or accountable to the electorate in any way. Quite the contrary, it is accountable only to a group whose interests are adverse to the electorate's. And second, the veto power of the union is not permanent, as it is in the case of elected officials. The fact that it is not permanent hardly changes the conclusion that public-sector-union veto power over the actions of publicly elected legislative bodies constitute an undemocratic sharing of public authority with a private group. And it takes little imagination to see what enormous damage would be done if special-interest groups in other fields had the legal power to delay changes in the laws affecting them, until they had dragged a public body through some sort of extended impasse procedure.

It frequently happens that an interest group drafts legislation that is later adopted by a public agency. At some point, however, public officials must adopt the proposed legislation as their own, but it can and often does originate with a private party. In this sense, the fact that many bargaining proposals ultimately adopted by a public employer originated with a union is not, prima facie, a change from accepted procedure in other areas of the policymaking process. Nevertheless, there is a difference that is enormously advantageous to public-sector unions and that exists nowhere else.

Previously, it was pointed out that the public employer is not legally obligated to agree to a union proposal or to make a concession. This is true, up to a point. The employer is not obligated to agree to any specific union proposal. On the other hand, the employer who agrees to none is likely to be in deep trouble for refusing to bargain in good faith. This issue is an extremely troublesome one in the labor-relations field generally, and some discussion of it is necessary here.

Under collective-bargaining statutes, the parties are required to bargain in good faith. Good faith is commonly interpreted as a sincere desire to reach agreement and an openminded attitude. Each side must be willing to consider the proposals of the other with an open mind. Essentially, good faith refers to a subjective attitude, which must be inferred from all the circumstances.

Suppose the union makes 100 proposals, all of which are rejected by the employer. Is such total rejection evidence of bad faith? It might be, depending on the circumstances. Theoretically, a union might submit 100 outrageous proposals. If it knew that the employer had to accept some in order to avoid charges of bad faith, that would be an encouragement for the union to submit scores of costly proposals, knowing that the employer had to accept at least a few. Of course, when an employer alleges that all the union proposals are unacceptable, the labor boards and the courts are caught in a dilemma. They cannot rule out of hand the possibility that the employer had good-faith reasons for rejecting all the union's proposals. Still the only way to determine this is to examine the union proposals and the employer's rationale for rejecting them. So doing, however, puts the agencies and the courts in the perilous business of dictating agreements or of forcing the parties to agree to a concession. As a federal court stated in a leading case upholding a decision by the National Labor Relations Board,

> It is true . . . that the Board may not "sit in judgment upon the substantive terms of collective bargaining agreements." But at the same time it seems clear that if the Board is not to be blinded by empty talk and by the mere surface motions of collective bargaining, it must take some cognizance of the reasonableness of the positions taken by an employer in the course of bargaining negotiations. . . .

> Thus if an employer can find nothing whatever to agree to in an ordinary current-day contract submitted to him, or in some of the union's related minor requests, and if the employer makes not a single serious proposal meeting the union at least part way, then certainly the Board must be able to conclude that this is at least some evidence of bad faith, that is, of a desire not to reach an agreement with the union. In other words, while the Board cannot force an employer to make a "concession" on any specific issue or to adopt any particular position, the employer is obliged to make *some* reasonable effort in *some* direction to compose his differences with the union, if §8(a) (5) is to be read as imposing any substantial obligation at all.[11]

When applied to public-sector bargaining, as it is in the bargaining-law states, the preceding quotation raises several basic issues. A public employer runs a significant legal risk in rejecting *all* union proposals. This risk is unique. In no other area does government come under such an obligation. If a city council rejected 100 proposals by developers, the latter could not charge the council with an unfair practice for refusal to consider its proposals with an open mind, in a sincere effort to reach agreement. Of course, the developers could make whatever political charges they wanted to in this situation, but they would have no *legal* basis for their charges.

Under bargaining, there is no obligation to accept specific union proposals but there is significant legal pressure to accept some of them. For this reason alone, the public-sector unions have the power to define issues to be voted on by public employers. Indeed, in the most fundamental sense, they have this power regardless since the public employer must adopt a position (accept, reject, or make a counterproposal) with reference to every union proposal made in bargaining.

As noted initially, our primary concern in this chapter was to be the process of public-sector bargaining, not the content of public-sector agreements. It is worth noting, however, that the procedural requirements in negotiated agreements often have an adverse impact on management. As one careful study noted, "At the same time, however, it was clear in many of the systems that the procedural or due-process requirements embodied in contracts had posed a serious if not insurmountable barrier for management in implementing some policy decisions and administrative actions.[12]

Public-Sector Bargaining as an Exception to Normal Political Processes

Suppose a city was about to adopt a land-use policy. It meets with representatives of the landowners' association but is unable to reach agreement. However, before the city council can act unilaterally, it must undergo mediation with the landowners' association. If mediation is unsuccessful, the differences are submitted to fact-finding, according to statutorily specified criteria. What would be the impact of such requirements on government generally? And if it be conceded that such procedures generally would accord far too much influence to special-interest groups, is there any reason to believe an exception should be made for public-sector bargaining?

At least one thoughtful observer has said that it should be. In his 1974 analysis, Summers explicitly accepted the political nature of public-sector bargaining. It was also clear that citizen exclusion from the policy-making process troubled him, but he accepted the fact that public-sector bargaining required an exception to the norms of democratic process. As Summers put it:

We must now confront the question whether the change worked by collective bargaining in the political process can be justified. Can we properly give public employees a special procedure that enables them to bargain separately from, and in some respects prior to, other interest groups in the budget—making process? Certainly giving one of several competing interest groups such a special status and role in governmental decision making is not in the pattern of our "normal" political processes and might be considered inappropriate in a democratic society.[13]

Summers subsequently commented:

Collective bargaining, however, does provide a special process available only to public employees and equally available to all classes of public employees. It significantly increases the political effectiveness of public employees in determining their terms and conditions of employment, particularly relative to other competing groups. . . . In my view, one of the principal justifications for public employee bargaining is that most public employees need this special process to give them an ability to counteract the overriding political strength of other voters who constantly press for lower taxes and increased services. . . . The significant questions in public employee bargaining are questions of governmental decisionmaking: By what process shall these important policy decisions be made, and by whom? The answers will not be found by comparing bargaining in the public sector with bargaining in the private sector, nor by asking what will facilitate bargaining. They will be found only by examining critically the impact of bargaining on the political process and asking what will improve that process within the premises of democratic government.[14]

Nonetheless, the issue is not whether the public employer bargains separately and/or prior to meeting with others interested in the same issues. It is the status of the agreements reached through such separate and/or prior bargaining and the effects of such agreements on participation by others in the policymaking process. Otherwise, however, Summers has formulated the crucial issues very well.

Previously, Summers argued that public-sector bargaining is a justified exception to our normal political processes for these reasons:

1. Employee payroll costs constitute 60 to 70 percent of most city budgets. Therefore wage increases inescapably lead to tax increases. This places public employees squarely in conflict with taxpayers as an interest group, with wage increases as the most visible and most vulnerable focal points for taxpayer opposition.

2. Employee demands for wage increases place them in opposition to other interest groups concerned about municipal budgets. These other groups want budget increases to provide more service; for example, more money for the police for more police protection. Higher wages for public employees, in and of themselves, result in less service. Other

things being equal, if you pay police higher wages, you have to employ fewer police. Thus the employee interest in higher wager places them in conflict with every group that wants increased services.

3. Public employees seeking wage increases tend to be isolated politically in this effort. They have "few natural allies and only limited ability to form coalitions." Even the support of organized labor is of questionable value in this context; private-sector members of labor unions are not necessarily supporters of higher taxes on themselves to pay for wage increases for their publicly employed brethren.

Because of these three factors, Summers concluded that public employees were unable to protect their interests adequately and that public-sector bargaining "seems an appropriate and necessary modification of the political process."[15]

Despite his noteworthy recognition of the basic issue, it is difficult to accept either Summers' conclusion or his rationale for it. Clearly, the notion that public-employee organizations cannot "adequately" defend the legitimate interests of public employees through normal political processes is highly debatable. The reader is again invited to review the list of statutory public-employee benefits in California—all of them enacted prior to that state's bargaining law. The list, incomplete as it is, hardly suggests inability to protect legitimate employee interests; if anything, it suggests inability of taxpayers to protect themselves from excessive employee benefits. Again, although the ability of public employees to achieve benefits varies from state to state, it must be emphasized that the bargaining laws have been enacted largely in the states that had also enacted the most extensive statutory benefits for public employees.

In the second place, the analysis ignores the advantages of public employment—including the advantage that support for political candidates results in a larger return for public employees than for nonemployees as a group. It is not that Summers analysis is wrong insofar as it goes. The problem is that he ignores or skirts over countervailing factors such as those discussed in previous chapters and elsewhere. Furthermore, one can readily accept the point that public employees have a unique relationship to public services, the tax structure, and/or the budget-making process. One can and perhaps should accept the idea that public agencies should deal with employee groups in some ways that are different from its relationships with nonemployee groups. Nonetheless, acceptance of these propositions does not necessarily justify public-sector bargaining. There are many other special relationships that might solve the problem without creating so many new ones and without involving such drastic change in democratic political processes.

Negotiating Schedules

Most state bargaining laws try to coordinate bargaining with the budgetary process. It was thought that in order to protect public employees from a fait accompli in bargaining, it should be completed prior to the adoption of the budget of the public employer. An oversimplified way of stating the conventional approach is that bargaining should dominate budgetary priorities; the latter should not dominate the bargaining.

Efforts to relate public-sector bargaining to budgetary processes have not been very successful. One obvious reason is that many high-priority union proposals such as binding arbitration or agency-shop clauses have no relevance to budgetary procedures or schedules. When impasse is reached on such items, the budget schedule is irrelevant, especially if the economic items are resolved. Even if they are not resolved, the unions are rarely concerned about the possibility that their constituents will suffer financially because there is no agreement by the date on which economic issues are supposed to be resolved. In other words, the budget-adoption date is not the critical point it was assumed to be—as evidenced by the fact that public-sector unions typically disregard it. Frequently the budget includes a reserve that includes the forthcoming wage increases. Often the public-sector union believes it can pressure the public employer to adopt a new set of priorities after the budget is officially adopted. This belief is often reinforced by the practice of inflating certain budgetary items to hide funds that can then be used for another purpose such as wage increases. Thus public employers frequently overestimate their needs for maintenance or supplies or services so as to conceal funds that can be used for employee benefits. Needless to say, many public-sector unions are not easily impressed by management assertions that the cupboard is bare.

For these and other reasons, efforts to coordinate bargaining schedule with budgetary ones have not been successful. They might be if the bargaining statutes did not mandate impasse procedures that extended beyond the budgetary schedule. A bargaining statute that accorded public employers the right to act unilaterally if no agreement was reached by a certain date (such as the budget-adoption date) could perhaps generate some pressure to bring about timely agreements. Public-sector unions would object to such legislation, but they could still be protected from bad-faith negotiations by means of unfair-labor-practice charges. If a public employer did not bargain in good faith prior to the date the employer could act unilaterally, the state PERB could require the employer to continue negotiations and/or to rescind the unilateral actions taken as a result of bad-faith bargaining.

Whether or not it is feasible to coordinate bargaining and budget making, the analysis here suggests a much different approach. The bargaining schedule should be coordinated with the schedule for electing the public officials who have the responsibility for approving or disapproving the agreements. Thus if a school-board or city-council election normally takes place the first Tuesday in November, the bargaining statute should provide that agreement must be reached by October 1 or the legislative body can act unilaterally. In other words, the bargaining schedule should frankly recognize the political nature of the public-sector labor agreement. By scheduling the termination of bargaining just prior to the appropriate election, it should be possible to generate and maintain a much higher level of awareness of the pros and cons of the public-sector agreement. It would be more difficult to hide collusion between public-management and public-sector unions since the proximity of elections would be a deterrent; individuals and groups not normally interested in public-sector agreements might well become very interested in them, as a potential campaign issue to be exploited in a rapidly forthcoming election.

Because personnel policies are such an essential component of public policies generally, it would be appropriate to complete action on the former just prior to the election involving the officials responsible for them. Bargainists are likely to be aghast at the suggestion, but the comment by Summers is apropos—the issue is not what will facilitate public-sector bargaining. It is what will improve the political process pursuant to which policy decisions are made concerning terms and conditions of public employment.[16]

Notes

1. Robert S. Summers, "Public Sector Bargaining Substantially Diminishes Democracy" *Government Union Review* 1 (Winter 1980):13. Reprinted with permission. This chapter especially, as well as several other portions of this book, owes a great deal to the Summers article just cited and to Robert S. Summers, *Collective Bargaining and Public Benefit Conferral: A Jurisprudential Critique* (Ithaca: New York State School of Industrial and Labor Relations, Cornell University, 1976).

2. *Abood v. Detroit Board of Education* (1977) 431 U.S. 209, 228.

3. An excellent analysis that makes this point very lucidly is Clyde W. Summers, "Public Employee Bargaining: A Political Perspective," *Yale Law Journal* 83 (1974):1156-1200. Incidentally, although recognizing collective bargaining as a political process, Summers nevertheless supported it in this article as a justified exception to normal political processes. See also Clyde W. Summers, "Public Sector Bargaining: Problems of Governmental Decisionmaking," *Cincinnati Law Review* 44 (no. 4) (1975):669-679.

4. Clyde W. Summers, "Public Sector Bargaining: Problems of Governmental Decisionmaking," pp. 669-679.

5. *Board of Education, Falconer Central School District No. 1 v. Falconer Education Association*; Case Nos. U-0599/D-0069, New York State Public Employment Relations Board, 24 May 1973.

6. *Department of Higher Education, Portland State University v. Morton H. Shapiro, et al.*, Oregon PERB, Case No. C-192-78, 25 April 1979.

7. Harry H. Wellington and Ralph K. Winter, "Structuring Collective Bargaining in Public Employment," *Yale Law Journal* 79 (April 1970):868-870.

8. U.S. Department of Labor, Labor-Management Services Administration, *Summary of Public Sector Labor Relations Policies* (Washington, D.C.: Government Printing Office, 1979), p. 65.

9. Quoted from Bureau of National Affairs, *Government Employee Relations Report* (Washington, D.C.: Bureau of National Affairs, 1972, No. 463, D-2 to D-6.

10. See Arvid Anderson and Joan Weitzman, "The Scope of Bargaining in the Public Sector," in Public Employment Relations Services, *Portrait of a Process: Collective Negotiations in Public Employment* (Fort Washington, Penn.: Labor Relations Press, 1979), pp. 183-184.

11. *NLRB v. Reed & Prince Mfg. Co.*, 205 Fed. 2d 131 (1st Cir.), cert. denied, 346 U.S. 887 (1953). For a comprehensive analysis of the good-faith issue in the private sector, see Gorman, *Labor Law*, pp. 399-496, especially 481-496.

12. Charles R. Perry, "Teacher Bargaining: The Experience in Nine Systems," *Industrial and Labor Relations Review* 33 (October 1979):16. Perry also noted that the public-sector agreements he studied often included formal consultation meetings that provided public-employee unions additional opportunities to extend their influence over personnel policies. Ibid., p. 14.

13. Summers, "Public Employee Bargaining: A Political Perspective," *Yale Law Journal* p. 1165. Reprinted with permission.

14. Clyde W. Summers, "Public Sector Bargaining: Problems of Governmental Decisionmaking," 675, 679. Reprinted with permission.

15. Summers, "Public Employee Bargaining: A Political Perspective," *Yale Law Journal* p. 1165-1168.

16. Summers, "Public Sector Bargaining: Problems of Governmental Decisionmaking," p. 672. For the view that labor-relations experts have ignored the political dimension to grievance arbitration in the public sector, see Peter Feuille, "Selected Benefits and Costs of Compulsory Arbitration," *Industrial and Labor Relations Review* 33 (October 1979):64-76. This issue is discussed in the following chapter.

5 Binding Arbitration of Grievances as a Policymaking Process

Thus far the analysis has focused on the procedures leading up to the public-sector labor agreement. We turn now to a discussion of grievance arbitration as a policymaking process.

At the outset, it may be helpful to review briefly the role of arbitration in labor disputes. Basically, arbitration is a procedure whereby an impartial third party makes a decision in a labor dispute. Arbitration may be *voluntary* (the parties have agreed to it) or *involuntary* (it is imposed upon the parties by law). Arbitration may also be *advisory* (the arbitral decision is recommended) or *binding* (the parties are bound by the decision). Binding arbitration is sometimes further divided into two additional categories: *final* (the parties cannot appeal the decision to the courts), and *binding but not final* (the arbitral decision is binding but can be appealed to the courts).

Essentially, two kinds of labor disputes may be subject to arbitration. One type is commonly referred to as "interest disputes," that is, disputes over what the terms of a labor contract should be. A situation in which the employer and union were at impasse over salaries for the coming year and agreed or were required by law to turn the dispute over to an arbitrator would be an interest dispute. Suppose, however, that the employer and union already have a contract covering salaries, but a dispute arises over what X should be paid pursuant to such contract. If X files a grievance alleging that he was not paid in accordance with the contract and if the grievance is ultimately carried to arbitration, then that procedure would be called "rights arbitration," that is, arbitration over the meaning, interpretation, and/or application of a labor contract.

Interest arbitration is not particularly widespread in the private sector, although it has its uses in certain kinds of situations. In the public sector its use increased substantially, especially in the 1970s. Thus by 1979 it appears that 30 states, 6 municipalities, 3 counties, and the District of Columbia had mandated binding arbitration of interest disputes.[1] As a rule, however, these statutes or ordinances provide that binding arbitration is applicable only to disputes involving security personnel: police, firefighters, and/or prison guards. The rationale was that these employees could not be permitted to strike; hence a fair procedure that provided finality was essential in

---

Portions of this chapter were first published in Myron Lieberman, "Binding Arbitration in Public Employment: A Reappraisal," *Government Union Review* (Spring 1980), pp. 33–41. Reprinted with permission.

their case. Nevertheless, interest arbitration encounters at least three problems in the public sector that do not apply to its use in private employment.

1. Permitting third parties not accountable to the electorate to resolve disputes over the terms and conditions of public employment is often regarded as an illegal delegation of legislative authority. A related argument is that the enacting bodies did not adequately spell out the criteria for arbitral awards; in fact, the statutes vary widely on this issue. As of 1979 appellate courts in five states had rejected these attacks and had accepted them (thereby invalidating the statutes) in three others.
2. Binding arbitration of interest disputes violates the one-man, one-vote standard mandated by the Fourteenth Amendment. Four state supreme courts have rejected this argument.
3. Binding arbitration of interest disputes violates state provisions relating to the powers of local governments. Obviously the validity of this argument depends on the state constitutions and statutes involved, but it is of some interest that appellate courts in three states rejected the argument and accepted it in two others.

No effort will be made here to analyze these legal arguments, many of which are still in litigation. As Rehmus points out, the basic issue is not legality but policy desirability. If binding arbitration is desirable, we can find a constitutional way to provide it. This of course is precisely the point made earlier about public-sector bargaining itself.

There is some evidence that compulsory interest arbitration does reduce the incidence of strikes—and that it results in settlements more favorable to the unions than would otherwise be the case. Weak unions tend to get more through binding arbitration than they would by efforts to exert pressure on public employers; strong unions can ignore strike prohibitions or use strike threats to stimulate higher awards. In addition, compulsory interest arbitration provides elected officials with a face-saving excuse to accept generous settlements that would boomerang politically if the officials proposed or endorsed them, rather than appearing to accept them reluctantly under pressure. There is also the danger in final-offer arbitration that the arbitrator may be forced to choose between two unrealistic positions. This can be mitigated by giving the arbitrator the authority to remand an issue to the parties for further negotiations; like most solutions, however, this one also creates or exacerbates some problems, such as the time devoted to bargaining and the additional restrictions on the public employer's ability to act.

Many persons who support binding arbitration of grievances in the public sector nevertheless oppose binding arbitration of interest disputes. Their opposition to interest arbitration is based on its impact on bargaining rather than on the political process. Interest arbitration is widely thought to "chill" the bargaining process. If the parties know that their dispute might be resolved by an arbitrator, they will not make many concessions or as many concessions during the bargaining. The reason is that arbitrators can be expected to make some concessions to both sides. If therefore you have already scraped the bottom of the barrel before going into arbitration, the only way the arbitrator can give the other party any concession is to award it a part of the barrel, that is, concessions that you cannot reasonably make.

To overcome this problem, some observers are urging the adoption of "final-offer arbitration" in interest disputes. In this process, the arbitrator is limited to choosing the final offer of either the employer or the union. This limitation is expected to stimulate bargaining and to avoid the submission of extreme proposals to the arbitrator; such proposals run a heavy risk that the arbitrator will select the final offer of the other party. Parenthetically, it may be noted that final-offer arbitration may be on either an issue-by-issue basis or restricted to the final comprehensive offers submitted by the parties. Regardless of its form, however, binding arbitration of interest disputes is a much more vulnerable process than binding arbitration of grievances. Let us see why even the latter is suspect.

In the private sector, grievance arbitration is a means of resolving conflict over the interpretation and application of a contract between private parties. Obviously disagreements over the interpretation and application of a contract arise in the public as well as the private sector. In the public sector, however, the disagreement is also and simultaneously a disagreement over the interpretation and application of a public law or policy having the force of law. This difference is crucial to the argument that follows.

As in the private sector, the grievance procedure is the focal point of contract administration. The terminal point of this procedure is frequently a troublesome issue. For example, public employers frequently object to grievance arbitration; their acceptance of it is often limited to advisory arbitration. On the other hand, public-employee unions typically object to advisory arbitration; in their view, advisory arbitration allows the public employer to decide unilaterally whether or not the contract has been violated. Some union negotiators actually prefer no contractual grievance procedure to one that provides for advisory arbitration.

Union arguments on this issue tend to regard a practical difficulty as a legal reality. Even under advisory arbitration, the public employer does not necessarily make the final decision on whether the employer has violated the contract. The union can still go into court to remedy an alleged violation. The time and expense required to do so, not the legal situation of the parties, underlies the union argument that the public employer (not the courts) is the terminal point under advisory arbitration. At one time or another, most citizens have probably waived their rights in a dispute because of the time and money required to enforce them. Undeniably, such situations exist and it makes sense to avoid them, insofar as reasonably possible. Thus the union argument may be correct as a practical matter, but nothing is gained, analytically at least, by treating the time and expense of litigating claims of contract violations as the absence of any legal right to such litigation.

About 95 percent of private-sector contracts provide for binding arbitration as the terminal point of the grievance procedure. As shown by table 5-1, public-sector labor contracts are characterized by more variation on this issue. Although binding arbitration is common and is certainly increasing in the public sector, the latter also includes many contracts with advisory arbitration, no arbitration, and even no grievance procedure at all. Binding arbitration is more common among the larger public employers, but all sorts of variations exist among public employers of every size. The high prevalence of binding arbitration in the private sector is frequently cited to justify its inclusion in public-sector contracts. What is often overlooked, however, is that binding arbitration did not receive instantaneous acceptance in the private sector; one study asserts that only 8–10 percent of private-sector contracts provided for arbitration in the 1930s.[2] Thus although a lower percentage of public-sector contracts include binding arbitration, its rate of acceptance may compare favorably with private-sector experience.[3]

Several factors underlie the greater variation in the public sector. The private sector is covered by a single law, the National Labor Relations Act. The public sector is governed by a multiplicity of state laws. These state laws differ widely in their treatment of grievance procedures. Some merely include such procedures as a subject of bargaining. Some require grievance procedures to be included in contracts. Some specifically aurthorize but do not mandate binding arbitration of grievances, and so on.

Timing is also a factor. Binding arbitration is the exception, not the rule, in first contracts after a bargaining law is enacted. Over time more public employers agree to the provision, and it becomes more difficult to hold out against it. Even so, many public employers continue to be opposed to binding arbitration; hence there is more variation in the alternatives to it.

In retrospect, it appears that many public employers have accepted binding arbitration of grievances as a result of their uncritical acceptance of the rationale for it in the private sector. According to this rationale, the arbitrator does not establish or create the terms of the contract. That is the responsibility of the employer and the union in bargaining. The arbitrator's task is to apply the agreement between the parties to a given set of facts in order to decide whether or not the employer has violated the agreement.

Table 5-1

Grievance-Arbitration Procedures by Level of Government

(In state and local government agreements, July 1, 1975)

					Level of Government					
	All Agreements		State		County		Municipal		Special District	
Procedure	Agreements	Workers	Agreements	Workers	Agreements	Workers	Agreements	Workers	Agreements	Workers
All agreements	624	788,233	69	270,281	281	208,350	234	274,325	40	35,277
Total with reference to arbitration	444	653,233	58	254,231	193	146,450	158	222,925	35	29,627
Advisory	35	42,800	—	—	27	21,900	7	19,100	1	1,800
Binding	351	516,683	53	244,831	133	66,725	132	177,375	33	27,752
Advisory and binding	33	57,075	—	—	26	51,025	7	6,050	—	—
Reference to arbitration, no details given	24	36,375	5	9,400	6	6,500	12	20,400	1	75
Other[a]	1	300	—	—	1	300	—	—	—	—
No reference to arbitration	180	135,000	11	16,050	88	61,900	76	51,400	5	5,650

Source: U.S. Department of Labor, Bureau of Labor Statistics, *Characteristics of Agreements in State and Local Governments,* 1 July 1975 (Washington, D.C.: Government Printing Office, 1977), p. 41.

[a]Includes one agreement in which the County Commissioners agree to binding arbitration only when the arbitrator's award does not exceed ¼ cent on the tax rate for a specific grievance or 1 cent on the tax rate in the aggregate.

Quite frequently the private-sector labor contract explicitly limits the arbitrator by language such as the following:

> The function of the arbitrator shall be to determine controversies involving the interpretation, application, or alleged violation of specific provisions of this Agreement, and he shall have no power to add to, subtract from, or modify any of the terms of this Agreement, or any other terms made supplemental hereto, or to arbitrate any matter not specifically provided for by this Agreement, or to enter any new provisions into this Agreement.

As more and more states enacted bargaining laws, there was increasing acceptance of the rationale for binding arbitration. The public-sector unions agreed that a collective-bargaining contract in the public sector is public policy, agreed to by the appropriate public employer. Nevertheless, they contended that an arbitrator ruling upon an alleged violation of the contract would not be *making* or *formulating* policy. The arbitrator would be merely deciding whether the public employer has acted consistently with the policy it adopted when it ratified the contract.

One argument was understandably ignored by the unions but inexplicably by public management. In the private sector, binding arbitration is usually a tradeoff for a no-strike clause. Prior to grievance arbitration, unions had serious problems attempting to remedy alleged violations of a contract. Quite often, their only recourse was a "grievance strike," that is, a strike during the term of a contract to force management to cease and desist violating it.

With a great deal of encouragement from the Supreme Court, management's acceptance of binding arbitration of grievances in the private sector became the accepted quid pro quo for the union's agreement not to strike during the term of the contract. This quid pro quo was not as advantageous to public- as it was to private-sector employers. The reason is that in most states, strikes by public employees were prohibited anyway, either by statute or judicial decision. For this reason, public employers would be giving the quid when they already had the quo. Undeniably, it was to their advantage to have the union's contractual agreement to a no-strike clause, but the private-sector tradeoff was clearly questionable just on bargaining grounds in the public sector. For the most part, however, public employers did not press the issue. Theoretically, public-sector unions might have made, or been asked to make, other concessions to justify binding arbitration, but this does not appear to have happened very often.

In any event, many public employers were (and are) very uneasy about accepting binding arbitration. It was almost as if they knew something was wrong but could not articulate their objections. Over and over again they had no effective response to the argument that the arbitrator would be deciding only whether the employer had violated its own policies. The unions also emphasized the argument that binding arbitration was needed so that the public employer would not be the final word on its own malfeasance. "Permitting one party to a contract to be the judge of whether it has violated the contract is unfair"; the unions have emphasized this argument since the inception of public-sector bargaining. Furthermore, in order to get binding arbitration, they were usually willing to accept contract language that restricted arbitrators, sometimes even more than was usual in the private sector. The following typical language illustrates this point:

> The Arbitrator shall limit his decision strictly to the application and interpretation of the provisions of this agreement and he shall be without power or authority to make any decision:
>
> 1. Contrary to, or inconsistent with or modifying or varying in any way, the terms of this agreement or of applicable law or rules or regulations having the force and effect of law;
> 2. Involving the exercise of discretion by the employer under the provisions of this agreement, under its by-laws, or under applicable law;
> 3. Limiting or interfering in any way with the powers, duties, and responsibilities of the employer under its by-laws, applicable law, and rules and regulations having the force and effect of law.

The Anomalies of Binding Arbitration in the Public Sector

Despite the wide acceptance of binding arbitration in the private sector, and despite union acceptance (at least initially) of restrictions on the authority of arbitrators there is something disingenuous about the argument for binding arbitration in the public sector. Why would a public employer argue against itself, that is, why would it try to violate its own policies while the union was simultaneously trying to uphold the employer's policy? It is almost as if a policeman were urging a violation of the law while the culprit is demanding that the law be enforced. As paradoxical as this would be, it is very similar to the outcome of binding arbitration in the public sector. The public-employee union alleges that the public employer is simultaneously denying paternity of the policy it allegedly adopted.

Of course, one can visualize situations in which a public employer deliberately wishes to deviate from its adopted policies. Management may believe that even-handed application of a policy would help an employee in disfavor or hurt an employee whom management desired to protect. Such instances do arise and are cited by public-employee unions to justify binding arbitration of grievances. Nevertheless, such cases are not the kind typically carried to arbitration. The typical case is one in which some consequences of a clear policy were overlooked, or a situation in which the contractual policy is not clear. For one reason or another, the public employer overlooked or was unaware of the application of the policy to a particular situation. Had it been aware of the lack of clarity or of the particular situation in which the policy is deemed inappropriate, the public employer would have negotiated a different policy.

Let us see how this happens. Suppose a school board agrees contractually to give salary-schedule credit for "five years of prior teaching experience." Let us assume that in the prebargaining years, the board has always interpreted and applied this phrase to mean public-school teaching experience. Assume also that contractual language provides that the contract supersedes any past practice that conflicts or is inconsistent with the contract. Subsequently, X files a grievance that is carried to binding arbitration. The grievance is based on board refusal to grant X five years' credit for X's teaching experience in a nonpublic school.

What are the realities of this situation? According to X, the board is violating its own policy by refusing to grant the five years of prior-service credit for teaching in nonpublic school. And true enough, the contract does not distinguish between public and nonpublic school experience; the board is violating the literal contractual policy by refusing to give X credit for teaching in nonpublic schools.

From a bargaining point of view, the resolution would be clear: X would get the disputed credit. From a public-policy standpoint, however, the case raises some different issues. It may well be that the board should have had a more astute negotiator or that the board was careless. Regardless, two things would follow from a binding arbitral award granting prior-service credit for nonpublic school teaching experience. First, the arbitrator would be *establishing* a public policy to which the public employer is opposed. Specifically, the arbitrator would be establishing the public policy that salary credit shall be given for nonpublic school teaching experience. It is disingenuous to argue that the arbitrator is merely interpreting but not formulating policy. In the absence of a collective-bargaining contract and binding arbitration, the board would not be forced to follow the policy that the arbitrator adopts and to which the board objects; the board could resolve any inconsistencies or ambiguities by adopting the policy it desires instead of being forced to adopt one promulgated by the arbitrator.

Note also that the grievance may arise as soon as the contract is ratified and that the arbitrator's decision may bind the board for years to an unwanted policy. It may also happen that dozens or even hundreds of teachers will benefit from this unwanted policy for this period of time.

To this observer, and I suspect to many others, it seems fair to say that the arbitrator is establishing board policy in this situation. For the sake of argument, however, let us adopt a different view. We shall say that the board established a policy it did not fully understand. Had the policy been fully understood, the board would not have adopted it—but the monkey is on the board's back, not the arbitrator's. The latter did not establish the policy; he only stated the consequences of it.

Even under this interpretation, however, it is clear that bargaining and binding arbitration of grievances result in public policies not desired by the community's elected officials responsible for them. It is evident that the basic issue is the same one discussed in the previous chapter. Under our normal political processes, the board at no time would have had to pay for the nonpublic school experience for any teacher. The discrepancy between the officially adopted policy and board practice would have been resolved by changing the officially adopted policy to conform to the intent of the board, that is, the responsible public agency. Under public-sector bargaining, however, the opposite happens; the policy not wanted by the board becomes operative, at least for the life of the contract and the duration of any impasse procedures thereafter. Even at that time, the board will presumably have to make some concessions on other matters to get rid of the policy it never wanted and never would have experienced except for public-sector bargaining. Which process then is to prevail? Either our normal democratic political processes take precedence over public-sector bargaining, or public-sector bargaining takes precedence over democratic political processes.

Binding Arbitration Limited to Factual Issues

Would it be feasible to limit binding arbitration in the public sector to factual issues? If feasible, such a limitation might be an appropriate way to avoid the policymaking dilemma otherwise inherent in binding arbitration in the public sector.

For instance, suppose a clerk at city hall is disciplined for cursing an irate taxpayer. The clerk grieves, asserting that the alleged cursing did not happen as asserted by management. In arbitration, the issue would be one of fact, not of policy interpretation. In fact, some contracts explicitly recognize this distinction by providing that an arbitrator can overrule management on the question of whether certain actions occurred but not over the appropriateness of disciplinary action taken if the acts did occur. *Example*: An employee is fired for stealing public property. Some contracts provide that the employee can grieve over whether the theft occurred but not over whether some lesser form of disciplinary action would be more appropriate.

Theoretically, it would be possible to have binding arbitration while avoiding arbitral policymaking by various restrictions on the arbitrator. Thus it might be agreed that arbitration would be binding only in disputes involving the resolution of a factual issue. Whether grievances can be categorized this way is questionable since both disputed facts and disputed policies are involved in many grievances. It would be possible to treat an arbitral decision as binding on factual issues and advisory on policy ones, but the outcome would be advisory arbitration in every case in which both elements were involved.

At least two problems with this solution should be noted. One is the possibility that the arbitrator would manipulate secondary issues to achieve an overall result desired by the arbitrator. Go back to our theft example briefly. Suppose an employee with 20 years' service was fired for allegedly stealing a pencil. Under the terms of the agreement, the public employer has the unqualified right to fire employees for theft. The arbitrator privately believes the employee did steal the pencil but that the firing was a harsh, even outrageous, result.

Did the employee steal the pencil? This would be a question of fact on which the arbitrator's decision would be binding. Obviously, the temptation would be great to rule against the city on the factual issue, thus depriving it of the right to fire the employee.

Could there be a dispute over whether an issue was factual or policymaking? As a practical matter, it is unlikely. However, assume it was an issue. The issue itself would have to go to arbitration. Such arbitration should probably be binding to be consistent with the logic of the solution.

The preceding compromise would probably be opposed by most public-employee unions. For those that have already negotiated binding arbitration without any limitations, it would indeed be a setback, however justified it would be on public-policy grounds. At the same time public employers that have already agreed not to limit binding arbitration of grievances are not likely to negotiate hard to bring about a limitation. Inertia is an important factor in labor relations. Once a public employer has accepted binding arbitration—especially in more than one contract—it would be extremely difficult for that employer to insist on the limitations suggested here.

Nevertheless, the limitation might enable public employers to avoid the most serious dangers of binding arbitration while nevertheless accepting it in a form that has some genuine utility for a union—and therefore would be more palatable than a complete rejection of binding arbitration. In any case, public employers that have not already agreed to binding arbitration of grievances have a valid public-policy reason for opposing or at least limiting such a concession. Needless to say, the unions are unlikely to concede that the preceding analysis has any merit at all.

Arbitral Bias as a Policy Issue in Public-Sector Grievance Arbitration

In a general way, policymaking in grievance arbitration is analogous to judicial legislation. Judges frequently have to interpret and apply legislation. When this happens, the judges are in effect acting as lawmakers. The argument over whether they are merely interpreting the law or formulating the law is largely a semantic issue. True, there must be some individual or agency with effective power to interpret the law. Furthermore, it would be foolish to argue that every judge is formulating the law, not merely interpreting it, in every judicial decision. The fact is, however, that the power to interpret the law is also the power to formulate the law.

By the same token, the power to issue binding interpretations of collective agreements is also the power to formulate such agreements, at least to a limited extent. And since such agreements constitute public policy for their duration, the power to make binding interpretations of them is a de factor power to make public personnel policy. A crucial difference, however, is that arbitrators instead of judges are making the public policy. It is one matter to recognize that ambiguities and inconsistencies in legislation are inevitable and to have a system for resolving them. In the judicial system, however, there is no inherent bias for or against any interest group. A judge who renders a decision in one case does not depend on the parties to accept him as a judge in future cases. Unfortunately, in grievance arbitration, the situation is precisely the opposite. This fact also raises several questions about the introduction of binding arbitration into the public sector.[4]

Arbitrators naturally deny that they are influenced by their acceptability in later cases. Their denials are based on the fact that there are losers as well as winners in arbitration. An arbitrator who ruled egregiously for a union to curry favor with it would be struck by management (in the next list, of course!) and vice versa. And since there is a mini-industry tracking arbitrators and arbitral decisions, arbitral performance allegedly has to convince both sides that the arbitrator is not influenced by the prospects for future selection as an arbitrator.

The fact that arbitrators must satisfy both sides over the long run is certainly an important consideration. It should be noted, however, that arbitral decisions can often go either way. Like judges, arbitrators often have opportunities to make decisions on one ground that is private and rationalize it on another ground that is public.

It can be conceded that not every arbitral decision jeopardizes the arbitrator's future acceptability to the parties. Nevertheless, such acceptability is more than a negligible consideration. This is reflected in the common practice of giving one party a favorable opinion and the other party a favorable decision. It is also reflected in the absence of arbitral criticism of frivolous grievances, that is, grievances that are obviously and completely without merit. Whereas judges peremptorily dismiss many frivolous lawsuits, arbitrators are more likely to act as if every grievance brought to arbitration is fraught with significance.

Arbitrators have a handy rationalization for this posture, to wit, the grievance procedure has therapeutic dimensions. It is therefore important to allow the union and the grievant to ventilate their frustrations in the procedure, even if the grievance obviously has no merit. Arguably, however, there is a causal relationship between the absence of such an attitude on the part of judges and the fact that they have heavy workloads and do not normally depend on the parties for continued employment.

One other bit of evidence that arbitrators are influenced by political considerations is that the unions act on the assumption that the arbitrators do have such concerns. An example may help to clarify this point. Unions often try to submit a number of grievances in a single submission or a single hearing. They hope that an arbitrator will feel a need to give something to each side. Therefore, instead of ruling for management in all cases—which would be the predictable outcome if each grievance were resolved independently—the arbitrator is more likely to sustain a grievance or two from the entire group.

For management to be in this situation, it would have to try to join several grievances that it was sure to lose in a single submission. This is unlikely to happen for at least two reasons. First, management is likely to sustain a grievance before arbitration if its chances of prevailing in arbitration are very poor. Second, management grievance decisions are not as subject to extraneous factors as are union grievance decisions. Unions are basically political organizations and their political needs—at least as perceived by union leaders—often require the processing of grievances that clearly lack merit. Facing a closely contested election, union leaders may submit all sorts of nonmeritorious grievances to convince members that the union is really active in their behalf. Management occasionally continues a grievance to arbitration for reasons that have nothing to do with the merits (for example, so that supervisors do not feel let down or for educational reasons), but this happens far less often.

Furthermore, the union is the moving party in grievance arbitration. It can control the number and timing of grievances to maximize its procedural advantages. Management cannot do this. Hence as a practical matter, relying on arbitrators to split decisions is a technique that helps unions much more than it helps management.

The upshot of all this in practical terms can be summarized as follows: (1) In public-sector bargaining with binding arbitration of grievances, public policy is often formulated and adopted by third parties not accountable to the public, and (2) the third parties involved are themselves an interest group with a stake in the expansion of public-sector bargaining and grievance arbitration.

The extent, if any, to which this predisposes their decisions in specific cases is debatable and involves many uncertainties and imponderables. The public employer can veto the choice of arbitrator up to a point—but not to the point of getting an arbitrator who is opposed to collective bargaining and grievance arbitration. Thus the impartiality of arbitrators is a relative matter. The question facing the employer is this: Among those who support collective bargaining and grievance arbitration, how is this individual likely to perform? To content that arbitrators must be impartial, else they would be boycotted by at least one party to the dispute, ignores the limited nature of the pool from which arbitrators are selected. When you strike arbitrators from a list, you are not saying that the names remaining are impartial or objective or competent. You are saying only that in your judgment, the arbitrators not struck from the list (and you cannot strike names ad infinitum) are a better risk than the ones who are struck.

Notes

1. Charles M. Rehmus, "Interest Arbitration," in Public Employment Relations Services, *Portrait of a Process* (Fort Washington, Penn.: Labor Relations Press, 1979), pp. 209-223. For data and legal analysis of binding arbitration of interest disputes, this discussion relies heavily upon the Rehmus study and Harry T. Edwards, R. Theodore Clark, Jr., and Charles B. Craver, *Labor Relations Law in the Public Sector*, 2d ed. (Indianapolis: Bobbs-Merrill, 1979).

2. Sumner H. Slichter, James J. Healy, and Robert E. Livernash, *The Impact of Collective Bargaining upon Management* (Washington, D.C.: Brookings Institution, 1960), p. 739.

3. For an account of the emergence of grievance arbitration in the public sector, see Gerald M. Pops, *Emergence of the Public Sector Arbitrator* (Lexington, Mass.: Lexington Books, 1975).

4. For a well-known criticism of grievance arbitration in the private sector and a rebuttal by an experienced arbitrator, see Paul R. Hays, "The Future of Labor Arbitration," *Yale Law Journal* 1019 (1965), and Saul Wallen, "Dispelling the Hays Haze," in *Proceedings, Eighteenth Annual Meeting of the National Academy of Arbitrators*, pp. 159-168 (BNA, D. Jones 1965).

6 The Constitutional Rights of Public Employees

The preceding chapters raised some constitutional and policy issues relating to the impact of public-sector bargaining on democratic political processes. This chapter raises similar issues relating to the impact of such bargaining on the individual and constitutional rights of public employees. Many of these issues could not reasonably have been foreseen until the 1970s, and their full ramifications are just beginning to be understood. One reason for this development is that the issues either do not arise or they have been resolved in the private sector. As we shall see, however, similar resolutions in the public sector pose several difficult constitutional and public-policy problems.

The basic problem can be summarized as follows: The Constitution provides public employees with certain rights pertaining to their employment status. In private-sector bargaining, these rights, if and when they exist, are subject to bargaining and hence to diminution or even extinction. In the public sector, however, these rights are personal and individual, as are most constitutional rights. For this reason, public employers and public-sector unions must be limited in bargaining. Otherwise, they could bargain away the constitutional rights of public employees. On the other hand, the fact that public employers and public-employee unions cannot make and enforce agreements that would be completely viable in the private sector clearly weakens the rationale for public-sector bargaining. As we shall see, the issues involved demonstrate basic differences between public and private employment that have yet to be fully confronted in public-sector bargaining.

In several cases, the U.S. Supreme Court has ruled that public employees, with certain limitations that are not relevant here, acquire a "property interest" in their public employment. The leading case is *Perry* v. *Sindermann* (1972) 408 U.S. 593. In this case, Sindermann, an instructor at Odessa Junior College, had been employed by the Texas State College System for 10 years. The college did not confer tenure on the faculty no matter how many years they had been employed.

In 1968 the college fired Sindermann without giving him a statement of the reasons or an opportunity to rebut the reasons. Sindermann sued, claiming that he had acquired an "expectancy" of reemployment that was a property interest. By firing him without providing the reasons or opportunity to rebut them, the college had deprived him of his property without due process of law. Such was Sindermann's claim—and it was upheld by the Supreme Court.

Note some fundamental distinctions between the outcome of the Sindermann case and the situation in private employment. A private-sector employee who had worked 10 years for the same company could still be fired at any time. No constitutional due-process rights accrue to the private-sector employee. Constitutionally, there is no expectancy of reemployment, and no employee property interest would be created by employment for a long period of time.

Another crucial point is that the public employee's property interest that is constitutionally protected extends to more than the job itself. For instance, a public employee probably could not be transferred arbitrarily and without notice from Odessa to Brownsville. Nevertheless, these property rights have not been precisely delineated. Some latitude must be accorded public agencies to manage their affairs; it cannot be that every time a public agency deprives a public employee of a benefit, it must provide due process for the employee. Nevertheless, uncertainty about the reach of the constitutional protection should not cause anyone to underestimate the enormous protection accorded public employees by Supreme Court decisions.

Let us now examine how these matters fare under collective bargaining in the private sector. As previously noted, unless limited by a collective-bargaining contract, employers have broad discretion to hire, fire, promote, demote, transfer, reassign, layoff, and so on. In bargaining, however, the employer and the union must distribute sacrifices as well as benefits. For example, suppose the parties are bargaining about layoffs. The union cannot protect every employee against a layoff. Therefore, it must agree to some provision that will resolve the order of layoff.

Typically, but not necessarily, the union will support seniority. Note that such a policy is inherently disadvantageous to some employees. More recent hires may want a lottery to decide who gets laid off. This is not fanciful or hypothetical. In recent years there have been frequent clashes between civil-rights organizations and unions over layoff procedures. The minority employees have frequently been the last hired. They contend that basing layoffs on seniority would destroy affirmative-action programs and result in disproportionate layoff of minorities. And in some cases, they have actually proposed that a lottery be used to decide who is laid off.

Other approaches are possible. "Eager beavers" among the employees may support an employer right to consider merit in layoffs. The crucial point is that whatever is negotiated, the union cannot avoid adopting a position that is better for some employees than others. If the union supports a lottery system, the senior employees who would keep their jobs on the basis of seniority will object.

Let us now add one more dimension to the problem. In bargaining, the union may be urging a wage increase that the employer is unwilling to grant. The employer may want the right to layoff through a lottery system that the union is unwilling to grant. Eventually, they may agree to a "bargain"—the general wage increase sought by the union in exchange for the employer's right to lay off through the lottery system. The union has a "duty of fair representation," which means that it must accord consideration to everyone it represents. However, such consideration does not preclude the union from agreements that hurt individual employees, as long as they are deemed in good faith to be beneficial to the majority. Thus in the preceding case, the union negotiators may believe the possibility of an actual layoff is not very great and that its agreement to the lottery was a good trade for the wage increase.

Problems essentially similar to these arise or can arise under virtually every issue subject to bargaining. A union proposal that every employee must join the union within 30 days after employment or be fired will hardly be perceived as beneficial by employees who do not want to join and pay union dues. A proposal that employees be promoted strictly according to seniority will be disadvantageous to employees who would be promoted faster under other criteria. And so on, ad infinitum.

It should now be clear that there is a basic conflict between collective bargaining and the constitutional rights of public employees. The private-sector union has the right to modify or even eliminate the same employee rights that are constitutionally protected in the case of public employees. For example, suppose there were collective bargaining in Odessa Junior College. The union representing professors might negotiate employer discretion in layoffs in exchange for several employer concessions.

For the sake of argument, let us concede that as most faculty view it, the contract is a good one. Nevertheless, the individual faculty member could not be deprived of his constitutionally protected property interest in his job—not even if every other faculty member at the college supported the agreement. The Supreme Court has frequently ruled that unions cannot negotiate away the basic statutory rights of employees set forth in Section 7 of the NLRA.[1] Thus it would be most unlikely to permit unions to negotiate away constitutional rights. As the Court stated in a leading First Amendment case, "One's right to life, liberty, and property . . . and other fundamental rights may not be submitted to vote; they depend on the outcome of no election."[2]

Policy Options

The clash between the imperatives of bargaining and the constitutional rights of public employees suggests at least three policy options:

1. Because the public-sector union and public employer cannot enforce an agreement that deprives public employees of their constitutionally

protected property rights in their employment, the parties to public-sector bargaining lack the flexibility to bargain effectively. On this view, public-sector bargaining would be undesirable public policy.

2. The process of collective bargaining in the public sector could be modified so that it would meet the constitutional requirements of due process whenever public employees lost constitutionally protected property rights.

3. Collective bargaining could be allowed in the public sector, but only agreements or the provisions thereof that did not violate constitutional rights would be upheld.

Of course, the first option would encounter all-out opposition from public-sector unions for whom it would be a "life-or-death" issue. It is not a viable option politically where public-sector bargaining exists—and there is no need for this additional rationale where it does not exist.

The second option seems as hopeless technically as the first one does politically.[3] To meet the constitutional requirements of due process, a procedure for depriving a public employee of his property rights would probably have to include the following:

1. Reasonable prior notice of any proposed action that would deprive an employee of a property interest.

2. A written statement of the proposed action and reasons for it.

3. Counsel to represent employee.

4. Right to examine and cross-examine witnesses.

5. A written record of the proceedings.

6. A written decision on the merits.

7. Some type of court review.

The Duty of Fair Representation

The idea that collective bargaining could be an adequate substitute for due process rests on the fact that the union has a duty of fair representation. However, the right to due process of law is a personal and individual right, which only the affected individual can waive; others may not waive these rights for the individual being deprived of this property. Even if this were not the case, it would be absurd to regard the union's duty to represent an employee fairly as equivalent to the employee's right to due process of law. This will be evident from a brief look at the former.

The duty of fair representation means that the employee must have a reasonably equal opportunity to participate in union affairs (speak at meetings, run for union office, and so on), and that the bargaining position of the union, or its handling of grievances must be based on good-faith consideration of the interests of all. This does not mean that the union cannot take a position disadvantageous to some of those it represents. As we have seen, this practice would be impossible. The point is that any union position taken that is disadvantageous to a group or individual represented by the union must have a reasonable basis. Thus a union need not process a grievance to arbitration if the costs would be great and the chances of winning very poor. On the other hand, it could not refuse to process a grievance because of racial discrimination or solely because the grievant was hostile to union leadership.

A brief look at some of the leading cases is instructive. The duty of fair representation was first enunciated by the Supreme Court in a case under the Railway Labor Act.[4] A railroad union negotiated several contract provisions that limited the number of black employees to be assigned certain positions and excluded them altogether from others. Black employees in the bargaining unit were prohibited from membership in the union, and some black firemen lost their jobs as a result of the agreement. The black plaintiffs filed suit against both the company and the union. The state court held against the plaintiffs, asserting that the union's power to bargain authorized it to agree to provisions that disadvantaged some employees. The Supreme Court reversed. Although not challenging the view that the union could act disadvantageously to some, such action could not be based on race. Also, since the black employees were not allowed to be union members, the court said that Congress could not have intended to strip the minority of all means of protecting its interests. Hence a duty of fair representation was inferred.

The next leading case involved a United Auto Workers (UAW) contract with Ford Motor Company.[5] The negotiated contract gave seniority credit for military service for employees who had not worked for Ford before the war. Since preemployment military service was not ordinarily a factor in accruing seniority, several employees who were disadvantaged by this provision filed suit, alleging that the UAW had violated its duty to represent them fairly. The Supreme Court refused to sustain the claim, asserting that the disputed provision was reasonably relevant and was reached in a good-faith effort to adjust the interest of employees in the bargaining unit. Note, however, that if this same issue arose in the public sector, the outcome might be different. Employees who are at the top of the seniority list if military service is not counted may have a property interest in that status. Seniority might be an important, even decisive, factor in promotions, rights to transfer, protection against bumping and layoffs, and so on. Therefore, it is questionable whether the union could bargain for a new basis for computing seniority.

Only two more of many interesting cases on this issue can be discussed. One case involved an employer whose workers were represented by the

United Transportation Employees (UTE).[6] The employer acquired another facility represented by the Teamsters. The employer and both unions agreed to conduct an election among the merged group to decide which union would be the exclusive representative.

Obviously, one of the bargaining issues to be faced by the winning union would be seniority. Normally, in such situations it is dovetailed, that is, employees in both locations are treated as if included in a single list. In this case, however, the UTE immediately campaigned on the basis that it would bargain for endtailing, that is, placing all the employees in the new facility (needless to say, the Teamster location, which had fewer employees) at the bottom of the seniority list. The UTE won the election, but the result was overturned by the court. It held that a union action, taken solely for reasons of political expediency, and without genuine effort to adjust the claims of employees at the smaller facility, violated the duty of fair representation.

One fact of crucial importance in this case needs to be emphasized. It shows that democratic procedures within a union do not necessarily result in the protection of individual rights. In fact, democratic internal process within the union might exacerbate a problem of individual rights. Union members are likely to vote their self-interest. Such self-interest may result in the majority's riding roughshod over the otherwise legitimate claims of a minority.

This point is dramatically illustrated by the last case to be considered.[7] In this case, a company concerned about continuing shortages in its cash receipts, proposed to fire all its employees as the most feasible way to solve the problem. The union persuaded the company to lay off half the employees; the layoffs were to become permanent if the shortfalls ended. When this actually happened, several of the permanently laid-off employees filed grievances over their layoffs. The union, however, refused to process the grievances, whereupon an employee permanently laid off filed suit against the union for violating its duty of fair representation. Significantly, there was no evidence that the plantiff had been dishonest or acted improperly. Nevertheless, the court did not accept the argument that the union had violated its duty of fair representation. It pointed out that the union had acted in good faith to benefit as many employees as possible.

For present purposes, the last point is crucial. Suppose this situation had involved a group of public employees, for example, employees at a city-operated lunch counter or recreational facility charging admission or toll-booth operators. Such employees have an individual constitutional right not to be deprived of their jobs without due process of law. The reasonableness of the union's action is hardly an adequate substitute for the employee's individual right not to be deprived of his property interest without due process of law. In our hypothetical example drawn from public employment, the public employer and union probably could not enforce an agreement similar to the one in *Union News*. That outcome, however, must be seen as a setback, not a gain, for public-sector bargaining.

A basic justification for collective bargaining is that it would encourage a more responsible attitude on the part of employees. In the absence of bargaining, everyone can pursue a "me-first" approach without regard to the rights and welfare of other employees. Under bargaining, however, the employees are forced to consider the situation from a larger perspective. If the employer's funds are limited, the union will have to adopt a position on how scarce funds are to be allocated.

For example, suppose the union's initial demands require a million dollars. Let us imagine the union proposed the following:

$500,000	General wage increase
$100,000	Longevity increase (sought by older employees)
$100,000	Reduction of steps to reach maximum (sought by younger employees)
$100,000	Early-retirement incentive plan
$50,000	Increase in extra-duty pay (to take care of the coaches and those who direct major school functions)
$100,000	Increase in insurance benefits
$50,000	Increase in leave benefits

Thus in the union's initial proposal, there are substantial benefits for everyone in the bargaining unit. In bargaining, however, it becomes clear that only $100,000 is available for wage and benefit increases. At this point the union must begin to share in the task of setting priorities. Unless it does so, there will never be an agreement. This is supposed to be helpful to the employer; if the union did not participate in setting priorities, the employer would face a large number of subgroups, each demanding benefits that would, if granted, force everyone else to go without any increase in benefits. Under bargaining, however, the union as well as the employer must defend and take some responsibility for the priorities reflected in the agreement.

The same principle applies when the employer experiences hard times. Bargaining becomes a matter of distributing sacrifices, not benefits. Suppose there is a drastic cut in the municipal budget. Layoffs are one alternative. Increased workloads are another. A wage freeze is still another. Eliminating certain services altogether may be still another. And so on. In the absence of bargaining, the employer is confronted by several groups, each of which wants some other group to bear the sacrifice. Bargaining supposedly minimizes this outcome because the union (which represents everyone) must share in the setting of priorities.

Let us now consider two public employers facing severe budget cuts. Employer *A* is in a state with no statutory benefits. Employer *B* is in a state with statutory benefits on every issue subject to bargaining. Clearly, Employer *A* and Union *A* have some freedom to bargain, although it will be limited by their need to respect the constitutional rights of employees. For example, it is doubtful whether they could bargain away job rights that are constitutionally protected, even though that might be part of the optimum solution from a bargaining point of view.

What about the situation with respect to Employer *B*? Here it is difficult to see how meaningful bargaining could take place. The parties cannot bargain a reduction of statutory benefits on any matter for anyone. Since it is impossible for the union to bargain on anything but an increase in benefits, the only concessions it could make would be to reduce its demands for increased benefits, say, from a 20-percent wage increase to a 15-percent increase.

Whether or not this can be considered collective bargaining, it can hardly be considered desirable public policy. Nevertheless, this was precisely the policy advocated by the Coalition of American Public Employees (CAPE) in its efforts to enact federal legislation providing bargaining rights for state and local employees.[8] In proposing such legislation, CAPE had to consider the effect of any such federal legislation on state legislation on terms and conditions of employment for state and local public employees. Normally, when Congress enacts legislation of this kind, it preempts state jurisdiction, that is, state legislation on the same subject is null and void. States have no authority to regulate interstate commerce; federal jurisdiction is exclusive, not concurrent. Similarly, in the labor-relations field, the states cannot legislate terms and conditions of employment that are subject to bargaining under the NLRA. To do so would interfere with the federally established rights of employers and unions to reach their own agreement on such matters.

Thus CAPE had a problem. If a federal statute providing public-employee bargaining rights were enacted and nothing was said about the state laws on retirement, tenure, leaves, and so on, the latter would be wiped out completely. Of course, this would have created an enormous national controversy in CAPE's constituent unions and their state and local affiliates. Imagine, for example, what would happen in the NEA and its state affiliates if the teachers in about 40 states learned that their own national organization had been responsible for federal legislation that eliminated their state tenure protections. CAPE solved the problem in a most ingenious way. Its proposed bill provided that:

> All laws or parts of laws of the United States inconsistent with the provisions of this Act are modified or repealed as necessary to remove such inconsistency, and this Act shall take precedence over all ordinances, rules,

regulations, or other enactments of any State, territory, or possession of the United States or any political subdivision thereof. *Except as otherwise expressly provided herein, nothing contained in this Act shall be construed to deny or otherwise abridge any rights, privileges, or benefits granted by law to employees.*[9]

The wording of the last sentence in 13(b) is so simple and appears so innocuous that its enormous significance can be (and was) widely overlooked. The effect of 13(b) would have been to preempt all state legislation on terms and conditions of employment *which was not an employee right, privilege, or benefit.* Thus a state law providing a *maximum* number of sick-leave days would be preempted, whereas a law providing a *minimum* number of such days would not be. In other words, every state law providing a limit or cap or restriction on public-employee benefits would have been preempted, that is, rendered null and void, if H.R. 8677 had passed. The public-employee unions would have been free to bargain for more but not for less than their statutory rights, benefits, and privileges.

In the private sector, the union has the power to diminish or reduce benefits because it has the responsibility for representing everyone in the bargaining unit; its responsibilities to the group as a whole may require that it accept diminution or even elimination of benefits for subgroups within the bargaining unit. If the public-sector union does not have the same power and cannot have it—because such power conflicts with the individual constitutional rights of public employees—should it have the same responsibility?

Any answer to this question must take into account the answer to still another question: What are the property interests of public employees that cannot be diminished or eliminated by the public-sector union? This is a complicated matter for two entirely different reasons. First, the Supreme Court decisions do not provide any clear-cut guidelines on the matter. Second, the property interests of public employees subject to constitutional protection vary enormously from state to state and even within states. This point requires clarification.

First, it must be recognized that the property interests that are constitutionally protected come from many different sources. They may come from a state constitution or a state statute. They may originate in a municipal ordinance or a school-board regulation. All these sources may provide benefits or rights that cannot be taken away from the public employee without due process of law. A simple analogy may be helpful. The money I have (clearly, not enough, but that is another problem) may be earned, inherited, given to me by relatives, paid from interest-bearing accounts, and so on. Regardless of its source(s), however, it cannot be taken from me by a public agency except by due process of law. Similarly, public employees may derive a property interest in their employment from a variety of sources. A federal statute may provide maternity benefits. A state constitution may provide retirement benefits. A state statute may provide leave benefits. A collective-bargaining agreement may provide still others. In all these cases, the source might have elected not to provide the benefit, that is, the property interest. Once provided, however, the individual public employee may not be deprived of it without due process of law.

In some situations, the practical effect is that it is impossible for a public employer to reduce a benefit once given. State retirement laws illustrate this. States often sponsor retirement plans that require employee contributions. In time the benefit levels may turn out to be excessive; hence the legislatures may act to reduce them. They cannot do so, however, with respect to current participants. The latter have a property interest in the current benefit level. Any statute that reduced this benefit level would run afoul of the Fourteenth Amendment, that is, would constitute deprivation of property without due process of law.

Here again we have a vital distinction between public- and private-sector employment that redounds to the advantage of public-sector employees. The benefit accorded public-sector employees may become a property interest such that it becomes virtually impossible to reduce or eliminate it. A benefit conferred in the private sector has no such constitutional status; hence there are no constitutional barriers to its reduction or elimination.

Bargaining Statutes and Statutory Terms and Conditions of Public Employment

As if the situation were not complicated enough, it is now essential to introduce some additional complicating factors. One is the fact that there may be state as well as federal constitutional protections against depriving public employees of a property interest without due process of law. Another is that the relationships between the state laws on terms and conditions of employment and the state bargaining laws vary:

1. Some bargaining statutes (for example, Connecticut, Hawaii, Iowa, New Hampshire) provide that nothing in the bargaining statute shall be deemed to supersede other state laws related to public employment.
2. Some bargaining statutes (about 15 altogether) provide that a negotiated agreement will take precedence over other statutes or administrative regulations.
3. Some bargaining statutes (for example, Michigan and New Jersey) are silent on the question of whether, in case of conflict, a negotiated agreement takes precedence over a statutory provision on a term or condition of employment. The state supreme courts have split on this issue; for

example, the Michigan Supreme Court upheld the provision in the negotiated agreement, whereas the New Jersey Supreme Court held that a negotiated agreement may not contravene specific state statutes, including civil-service cases.

4. Some states have enacted different bargaining laws to cover different categories of state and/or local employees. For example, California has separate legislation governing employment relations in school districts, agencies of the state government, local governments other than school districts, and higher education. The bargaining statute governing public-school employees prohibits a collective agreement from superseding other legislation on terms or conditions of employment, whereas the bargaining statute for state employees expressly permits a negotiated agreement to prevail over other statutes and state administrative regulations.

To see the importance of the issue, suppose a state has a tenure law for public-school teachers. It enacts a bargaining law that says nothing about the relationships between the tenure law and any collective agreements reached pursuant to the bargaining law. Let us suppose that both a teacher union and a board of education prefer a negotiated tenure policy that is different from the statutory one. Do the parties have the authority to negotiate such a policy and have it prevail over the statutory one? In state after state, nobody knows the answer to this question and countless others like it. It would appear, however, that if such a negotiated provision were less advantageous than the tenure law to a particular teacher, it would deprive that teacher of his property without due process of law. In other words, the negotiated provision would be null and void insofar as it applied to teachers who would be better off under the tenure law; depending on circumstances (such as whether the agreement included a severability clause), the entire agreement might be null and void.

The constitutional dilemmas of public-sector bargaining are most easily seen in states that (1) provide a substantial number of statutory benefits for public employees, and (2) permit a negotiated agreement to supersede a conflicting statute. In this situation, public-sector bargaining raises the possibility that public employees can lose the statutory benefits without due process of law (except, of course, on the assumption that public-sector bargaining itself constitutes or is equivalent to due process of law. Perhaps the best way to clarify the issue is to examine an actual case in which this precise constitutional issue was raised. California's State Employer-Employee Relations Act (SEERA) provides that agreements between unions of state employees and the state government will take precedence, "without further legislation," over 137 provisions of the State Civil Service Act. Among the provisions are the following:

Sections	18300 18301 18302 18310	Provides Workmen's Compensation Law benefits for death or disability and defined firemen's activities under which benefits may be paid.
Section	19261	Authorizes the SPB to establish health-and-safety standards and to develop health-and-safety programs in state agencies.
Section	19332	Provides guidelines for employees on temporary or permanent disability; employee's rights to return to his former position; obligations of the appointing power of the SPB to place the employee in another position; employee salary rights upon transfer or demotion.
Section	19334	Permanent female employee rights to have up to a full year's leave of absence for pregnancy.
Section	19335	Provides for certificated employees to accumulate educational leave, with pay, at the rate of 1¼ days for each month served. Requires the SPB to provide rules for accumulation, regulation, and transfer of such leave.
Section	19360	Grants employee rights to notice and reason for transfer.
Section	19361	Permits employee to seek SPB review of transfer made to discipline or harass him.
Section	19452	Requires appointing power to counsel and train employees whose positions are being substantially changed or eliminated and requires the SPB to plan and to cooperate with the appointing power in retraining and placement.
Sections	19460- 19465	Grants employees up to $250 per year for uniform replacement. Grants certain employees work clothes. Grants employees safety equipment and police protective equipment required by the employing state agency.
Section	20750.11	Requires state to contribute 0.13 percent of compensation paid to state members, other than school members, for insurance benefits under the group term-life-insurance system.
Sections	21400 21402 21404 21405	Provides group term-life-insurance benefits to certain members of the system; outlines conditions of payment, amount of benefits, and state contributions.
Section	22754	Provisions and definitions relating to employee, employer, contracting agency and employee annuitant with regard to health benefits.
Section	22816	Grants employee entitled to a health-benefit plan the right to continue health-benefit coverage during a leave of absence without pay or other comparable leave.

Section   22825   Describes contributions by employer, employee, and annuitant to state health-benefit plans.

The preceding list is not exhaustive, but it does suggest the importance of the benefits, which could be reduced or eliminated in bargaining under SEERA. Such reduction or elimination, moreover, could occur without any regard for the constitutional rights of the employees affected thereby. As we have seen earlier, it would be unrealistic to contend that the union's duty of fair representation is the constitutional equivalent of due process of law.

The possibility of negotiating for less than a statutory benefit raises an interesting policy issue and bargaining problem. In the 15 states in which a negotiated agreement supersedes a conflicting statute, public employers can presumably bargain for less than the statutory benefits; otherwise, it would be pointless to refer to a conflict between the negotiated agreements and the statutes. The public employers who provide more than they are required to do by statute are not deemed to be in conflict with it. A conflict arises when a public employer bargains for benefits less than are provided by statute. Initially at least, the union will probably reject any such substatutory level of benefits, even on a single issue.

In this situation, the union could avoid any reduction of the statutory benefits simply by refusing to accept any in the agreement. By the same token, however, the public employer might avoid an agreement by refusing to accept any without any reduction of statutory benefits. Of course, the union would charge the public employer with bad-faith bargaining in this situation, but there is no prima facie reason why the employer's refusal to accept an agreement without a diminution of statutory benefits should be any more bad faith per se than the union's refusal to accept an agreement that includes such diminution.

Whether an agreement that deprives individual public employees of nonbargaining property rights in their positions is constitutional has yet to be resolved; undoubtedly, this issue will eventually reach the U.S. Supreme Court. A California case currently being litigated raises precisely this issue; however, because of the circumstances of this particular case, it is unlikely to be heard in federal courts for several years.[10]

We have yet to consider the other horn of the constitutional dilemma—the one most likely to be the reality that must be faced. Let us assume that public-sector unions cannot deprive public employees of any constitutionally protected property interest. Again it must be emphasized that even if the public-employee union, the public employer, and the vast majority of employees in the bargaining unit agreed on a provision that deprived a public employee of a constitutionally protected property interest, it could not be implemented over the objections of a single affected employee. By the same token, however, the public-sector union and public employer are precluded from fulfilling a major function of bargaining. They cannot effectuate a comprehensive adjustment of the interests of employees in the bargaining unit.

Unfortunately, the significance of such a limitation on bargaining was not considered in the enactment of the state public-sector bargaining statutes. Even in the states with extensive statutory benefits—in fact, primarily in such states—public-sector bargaining was superimposed on the statutory rights, benefits, and privileges of public employees. The fact that this additive approach is fundamentally inconsistent with the rationale for collective bargaining naturally does not trouble the public-sector unions. They are understandably delighted with the inconsistency; it means that they can bargain for more than the statutory and constitutional benefits, but never for less. And where, as is often the case, the statutory benefits are rather substantial, the result is that the point of departure in bargaining is an extremely high benefit level.

Policy Recommendations

Although the constitutional issues are important, they are secondary to the public-policy issues. The reason is that we can find a legal way to implement desirable public policy. Partly for this reason, the legal arguments here are not exhaustive and not intended to resolve the policy issues. Instead, they are intended to clarify policy issues that will have to be confronted with increasing urgency in the 1980s.

In light of the issues discussed in this chapter, the policy argument for public-sector bargaining must be questioned, especially in states with extensive statutory benefits for public employees. Inasmuch as these are the states in which the public-sector unions are the most influential politically, the outlook for repeal of either the statutory benefits or the bargaining statute is not very promising; nevertheless, if there is to be public-sector bargaining, state legislatures should consider the following options:

1. Repeal the state statutes on terms and conditions of employment for public employees. This would remove a built-in bargaining advantage of public-sector unions and provide a clean slate for bargaining.
2. Exclude from the scope of bargaining any matter covered by a state statute. Thus if a state statute mandated 10 days' sick leave annually for public employees, public employers should not be required to bargain on proposals to provide more than 10 days. The logic would be that since the parties cannot bargain for less than the statutes provide, the public employer should not have to bargain for more. Minimally, state legislatures should insist that public employees waive any bargaining rights on matters covered by new legislation. Such insistence would

help to take the legislatures out of the business of legislating terms and conditions of public employment that should be resolved locally. It would also help to end the indiscriminate resort to both statutory and contractual systems of benefits.

3. As an alternative to (2), above, a legislature might provide that if a public-sector union proposes to bargain for more than a statutory benefit, the public employer shall have the right to bargain for less and to implement less if no agreement is reached. This provision requires that a negotiated agreement take precedence over a statute on the same subject. As we have seen, such provisions may not withstand constitutional challenge.

4. From a bargaining point of view, the danger that a diminution of employee rights established outside of bargaining would encounter a constitutional challenge should be considered carefully.

The public employer may have to reject a standard severability clause and specify what would happen if a contractual agreement to reduce statutory employee benefits were invalidated. This precaution may be especially useful in the states that permit the negotiated agreement to supersede statutes that conflict with them.

Organizational Security in the Public Sector

Union-unit member relationships in the public sector are clearly affected by some constitutional and policy considerations that do not apply, or apply in a different way, in the private sector. This is evident from an analysis of various issues pertaining to organizational security. It is too early to assess the full significance of the differences, but it is already clear that wholesale application of private-sector law and rationale simply ignores the political dimension to public-sector bargaining.

In the private sector, the employer and union can adopt and enforce a clause requiring unit members to join the union 30 days after the effective date of an agreement. Section 8 (a)(3) of the NLRA specifically authorizes such provisions in the following language:

> Nothing in this Act . . . shall preclude an employer from making an agreement with a labor organization . . . to require as a condition of employment membership therein on or after the thirtieth day following the beginning of such employment or the effective date of such agreement, whichever is the later . . . .

The NLRA was amended in 1947 to include, inter alia, the highly controversial Section 14(b), which reads,

Nothing in this Act shall be construed as authorizing the execution or application of agreements requiring membership in a labor organization as a condition of employment in any State or Territory in which such execution or application is prohibited by State or Territorial law.

Subsequently, an employer in a right-to-work state refused to bargain on an agency-shop clause. Such a clause does not require unit members to join the union, but it does require them to pay a service fee to the union for negotiating and administering the contract. The union filed charges of refusal to bargain. The employer's position was that since the agency-shop clause did not require membership in the union, it was not authorized by the NLRA; only agreements requiring membership as a condition of employment were authorized by 8 (a)(3).

In its decision, the Supreme Court treated the payment of union fees and dues as the equivalent of membership in the union. The Supreme Court decision held that:

It is permissible to condition employment upon membership, but membership, insofar as it has significance to employment rights, may in turn be conditioned only upon payment of fees and dues. "Membership" as a condition of employment is whittled down to its financial core.[11]

In another case decided the same day, the Supreme Court held that Section 14(b) gave the states the right to override agency-shop clauses on the basis that such clauses were the equivalent of a membership requirement.

Let us add one more dimension to union-security issues before turning to their public-sector implications. Over the years dissident union members have frequently protested compulsory membership in, or compulsory financial contributions to, unions as interference with their freedom of thought, conscience, and expression. Although the First and Fifth Amendments prohibit only action by the federal government, the Supreme Court has ruled that agreements pursuant to Section 8(a)(3) of the NLRA may be considered action by the federal government in certain circumstances. On this basis, dissident employees contended that in order to keep their jobs, they were required in effect to support political candidates and doctrines to which they were opposed. In a leading case on the issue, a divided court held that although unit members could be assessed a fee to defray the costs of negotiation and administration of the collective agreement, the union could not, over an employee's objections, use a portion of the employee's dues money for "political causes."[12] In a 1973 case, a federal district court attempted to clarify "political causes," stating:

Dissenting employees in an agency fee situation should not be required to support financially union expenditures as follows:

One, for payments to or on behalf of any candidate for public office in connection with his campaign for election to such public office, or

Two, for payments to or on behalf of any political party or organization, or

Three, for the holding of any meeting or the printing or distribution of any literature or documents in support of any such candidate or political party or organization.

[E]xpenditures for other purposes . . . are sufficiently germane to collective bargaining to require dissenting employees who are subject to union shop or agency fee agreements to bear their share of that burden.[13]

This entire chain of private-sector precedent has frequently been adopted in toto by state PERBs. Whether it is constitutional to do so and whether it makes sense even if constitutional are other matters.

At the outset, it should be noted that the claim that all unit members benefit from union representation is open to challenge. As might be expected, the issue is an extremely controversial one in the labor-relations field. To this observer, the claim is an empirical one that is true (and false) in varying degrees, from bargaining unit to bargaining unit and contract to contract. Regardless, even if all unit members benefit in particular situations, it would not necessarily mean that everyone benefits to an amount or degree equal to the cost of such benefits to the unit members.

Actually, it is hardly debatable that not everyone benefits equally; the previous discussion relating to the duty of fair representation should be dispositive of that issue. Indeed, decertification petitions would be inexplicable if all unit members benefited, or benefited equally, from union representation. At best, therefore, the rationale for agency-shop clauses is vulnerable to both theoretical and empirical challenge. The following analysis does not challenge the rationale for agency-shop clauses in the private sector but is intended only to raise some questions about its applicability to the public sector. In doing so, there is no intent to express approval or disapproval of its existence in the private sector or to convey the impression that its existence there is not being challenged.[14]

First of all, the distinction between bargaining and political expenditures hardly makes sense in the public sector. In bargaining, the public-sector union is trying to persuade the public employer to adopt a set of public policies. As numerous authorities cited in this study have said, public-sector bargaining is a process of establishing public policies—that is, policies that, like any others adopted by a public body, are inherently political. As Justice Powell noted in his perceptive dissent in the Abood case (see p. 70), the only difference between a public-sector union and a conventional political party is that the public-sector union typically focuses on a much narrower range of issues—those relating to terms and conditions of public employment. For this reason, the effort to distinguish between bargaining and political expenditures by a public-sector union is doomed to fail. It assumes that the distinction between bargaining and political expenditures makes sense, or as much sense, in public- as it does in private-sector bargaining. In the opinion of this observer, it does neither.

By the same token, it hardly makes sense to prohibit public-sector-union expenditures for political doctrines opposed by some union members. What sense does it make to require a public employee to contribute to the costs of negotiating policies with which he disagrees but not to require him to contribute to political campaigns intended to achieve the same result? For instance, suppose a group of public employees are opposed to reliance on seniority in layoffs. Under an agency-shop clause, these employees must nevertheless contribute to the union effort to negotiate just such a clause. Suppose further that of two candidates for mayor (who is responsible for the management position in the negotiations), one supports and one opposes the union's position. It would be a triumph of terminology over substance to argue that there is any significant difference in these situations from the standpoint of the rights of dissident union members. This is especially evident when one takes into account the dynamics of public-sector bargaining. The union frequently castigates public management as harshly as possible in order to put more pressure on it to accept union demands. And so the union alleges publicly that management is "hardnosed," "not bargaining in good faith," "does not care about employees," "is subservient to the big taxpayers," and so on. Such charges are intended to bring about changes in public policies identical to those sought in election campaigns. Paradoxically, employees could be required to pay for such an advertisement as part of the union's bargaining effort; they could not be required to pay for the identical advertisement in an election for public office. And if the bargaining is being conducted in close proximity to an election, the absurdity of the bargaining-political dichotomy, at least as it affects public-sector-union dues, is even more evident.

If one adheres to the view that union dues and fees ought not be devoted to political purposes over the objections of employees forced to contribute, public-sector unions should be denied agency-shop fees or any other form of compulsory contributions from public employees. Alternatively, it would also be consistent to ignore the distinction between bargaining and political action in the case of public employees and to permit agency-shop fees to be used for political as well as bargaining purposes. The alternative that appears to make no sense (or makes the least sense) is the one adopted in most states, that is, authorization of agency-shop fees but not contributions for political purposes.

Previously it was noted that the Supreme Court, in ruling that agency-shop fees were negotiable, regarded them as compulsory membership, "whittled down to its financial core." It is somewhat anomalous therefore to see how often agency-shop fees have been authorized by statute or upheld by state courts because they do not require public employees to join a union to keep their jobs. In any event, agency-shop fees create a dilemma for public employees. On the one hand, the employee can pay the agency fee, knowing that it will be used to promote political positions opposed by the employee. The fact that these positions are labeled "bargaining positions" in no way changes their essentially political nature in the public sector. Furthermore, by paying only the agency-shop fee, the employee loses the right to participate in the internal affairs of the union and thereby change its policies or leadership. Freedom not to pay anything would provide some leverage, whereas compulsory payment of an agency-shop fee deprives the employee of most of his influence over union policy.

The alternative is to pay the dues and fees and participate, if possible, in union affairs. The difference between the agency fee and full-membership dues and fees may or may not be large; just how large was in litigation in 1980. Because the agency fee (by statute or court decision) typically amounts to 80 to 100 percent of bargaining-agent dues, the saving to the employee lies primarily in the fact that the employee need not pay the dues of regional, state, and national affiliates of the bargaining agent. Full membership usually entails payment of such dues, and they are usually much larger than the difference between local dues and the service fee.

Also the membership option assumes that the unit member who wants to influence union policy can and will be active in union affairs to exert such influence. This is not a realistic assumption for many unit members. Even when such activity is possible, it often has no realistic chance of changing anything. (See the discussion at the end of chapter 1.) In short, the public policy justification for forcing public employees or allowing them to be forced to choose between two distasteful alternatives has yet to be demonstrated.

In a critical analysis of the Supreme Court decision in the *Street* case, Wellington points out that even as applied to private-sector unions, the Court's efforts to distinguish between bargaining from political activities is unsound.[15] Wellington suggests that Congress make it possible for private-sector employees to opt out of certain union political activities and to receive an appropriate rebate of union dues if such option were exercised. The latter would not, however, apply to political activities related to collective bargaining. In the public sector, the extent to which such a policy would legitimize union political expenditures over member objections would vary enormously, depending on the state legislative standards and the way they were interpreted and enforced.

Notes

1. *Wallace Corp. v. NLRB*, 323 U.S. 248 (1944); and *Radio Officers v. NLRB*, 347 U.S. 17 (1954).

2. *West Virginia State Board of Education v. Barnette*, 319 U.S. 624 (1943).

3. See, however, James Baird and Matthew R. McArthur, "Due Process and Arbitration Problems," in *Bargaining*, ed. Myron Lieberman (Chicago, Ill.: Teach Em, Inc., 1979), pp. 171-178.

4. *Steele v. Louisville & Nashville Railroad* (1944) 323 U.S. 192.

5. *Ford Motor Company v. Huffman* (1953) 345 U.S. 696.

6. *Truck Drivers Local 568 v. NLRB (Red Ball Motor Freight, Inc.)* 379 F.2d 137 (D.C. Circuit, 1967).

7. *Union News Company v. Hildreth*, 295 F.22 658 (6th circuit 1961), cert. denied 375 U.S. 826 (1963), 712.

8. CAPE is a confederation of public-employee unions that includes the National Education Association, the American Federation of State, County, and Municipal Employees, American Nurses Association, National Treasury Employees Union, National Association of Social Workers, and Physicians National Housestaff Association.

9. *Section 13(b), H.R. 8677, 93rd Congress.* Italics added.

10. See *Pacific Legal Foundation et al. v. Edmund G. Brown, Jr., Governor of the State of California et al.*, 3 Civil No. 18364 and 3 Civil No. 18412, Third Appellate District, Court of Appeal of the State of California, 25 March 1980.

11. *NLRB v. General Motors*, 373 U.S. 734 (1963).

12. *IAM v. Street*, 367 U.S. 740 (1961).

13. *Seay v. McDonnell Douglas Corp.*, 371 F. Supp. 754, (C.D. Cal. 1973).

14. See Gorman, *Labor Law*, pp. 639-672, for an excellent discussion of union security in the private sector. For a strong criticism of agency-shop clauses in the private sector, see Philip D. Bradley, *Constitutional Limits to Union Power* (Washington, D.C.: Council on American Affairs, 1976).

15. See Harry H. Wellington, *Labor and the Legal Process* (New Haven, Conn.: Yale University Press, 1968), pp. 239-265.

7

The Costs of Public-Sector Bargaining

This study has frequently criticized statements or claims made about public-sector bargaining. Let us now turn to a remarkable analytical gap concerning it, to wit, the absence of data on or analysis of the cost of the process. I am not referring to the costs required by negotiated contracts but rather to the costs of the negotiating process itself. From 1960 to 1978, not a single article on the costs of public-sector bargaining was indexed in the periodical literature on labor relations. Since then, the literature has been sparse indeed. Kerchner conducted a study of the 1977 costs of bargaining in California school districts. He estimated the costs to school districts alone to be $35 million more than their meet-and-confer costs. His estimate omitted state costs, union costs, and the value of contributed services on both sides such as the time of school-board members and union negotiating teams.[1]

Gearhart and Krolikowski studied the costs of bargaining in four cities, two in the East and two in the Midwest. Their population ranged from 33,000 to 104,000. It was estimated that bargaining costs in 1975 ranged from $76,000 to $91,000. The researchers specifically disclaimed any value judgment on these amounts but were impressed by the similarity of the costs despite the different governmental structures involved and the different legal and political contexts in which municipal bargaining took place.[2] Surely, however, the cost of a decision-making process is an important dimension of its feasibility. We can hardly avoid cost considerations in recommending a system for making public policy or resolving disputes between public employers and public employees. Nevertheless, I was able to locate only one study that not only raised the question of whether the costs of public-sector bargaining are worth the benefits but that also made several specific suggestions to reduce the costs. This publication was sponsored by an Oregon foundation composed predominantly of business leaders.[3] Mention should also be made of a recent Canadian publication that includes some incisive comments on the costs of bargaining in Ontario school districts.[4]

Here again the passage of time is relevant. In 1960 the absence of cost data would have been thoroughly understandable. Public-sector bargaining was limited almost entirely to a few large cities. Had data on bargaining costs in these cities been available, they probably would have been of no interest to the vast majority of the 80,000 public jurisdictions at the time.

In fact, the data would have been misleading since the costs under a bargaining statute can be very different from the costs of bargaining in the absence of a statute.

What could be ignored in 1960, however, requires some explanation today. What are the costs of the process? The costs of public-sector bargaining are admittedly difficult to ascertain. Budget categories provide little help. For example, one city may employ a director of personnel who devotes half his time to bargaining and grievance processing. Another city of the same size may employ a labor-relations attorney to negotiate; the fees may be billed as legal fees. Still another city may assign bargaining to various agency heads, who by choice or assignment devote varying amounts of time to the process.

As the size of the bargaining unit increases, more costs are scattered through more departments. The negotiator may make substantial time demands on the business office for payroll or leave data or for projections of the costs of various union proposals. Demands for secretarial time increase—proposals and counterproposals must be typed and distributed, votes taken and typed and reproduced, agenda's prepared, communication with principals maintained, and so on. Memory is notoriously unreliable, but it is about all there is to estimate costs for those who are not employed full time in the negotiations process.

The direct and indirect costs of grievance procedures must also be factored in, especially if arbitration is the terminal point of the procedure. Grievances may involve the paid time of a grievant, the grievant's representative(s), and witnesses as well as the time of appropriate administrative personnel; if arbitration is invoked, attorneys are likely to be involved. A day devoted to preparation, a day at the arbitration hearing, and a day to prepare a posthearing brief and rebut the union's, could easily cost $1000 just for the attorney fees.

Public employers frequently have no control over some of the most important factors related to costs. Other things being equal, a bargaining statute that encourages unit fragmentation will result in larger costs than a statute that favors inclusive "wall-to-wall" units. Statutes that mandate extended impasse procedures, including fact-finding, also tend to result in higher costs. California statutes require public employers to provide "a reasonable amount of released time" for union representatives to negotiate and process grievances; many a California public employer has spent substantial sums in released time just to negotiate what is "a reasonable amount of released time" under the statute.

Accurate data on costs would have to take into account the costs over a period of time. The negotiating costs per year of a three-year contract are usually less than the costs per year associated with a two-year contract; a similar relationship usually exists between the costs of two- and one-year contracts.

Costs and Bargaining Outcomes: A Case Study

Cost factors often have a greater impact on the outcome of negotiations than is generally realized. An actual case involving a school district may help to explain. In 1976 the union representing classified (nonteacher) employees submitted a 132-page list of proposals. The district was the first large district in the area, and one of the first in the state, to be negotiating under the state's newly enacted bargaining statute.

As the district viewed the matter, it had reservations about the negotiability of 19 basic union proposals. Some could be categorized as clearly outside the scope of bargaining. Others were probably outside the scope of bargaining; still others were arguably outside the scope, but the district would probably lose a legal challenge to most proposals in this latter category. Before reviewing the internal board discussion, it should be noted that the bargaining statute specifically provided that a public-sector employer may not meet and negotiate on anything not stated to be within the scope of bargaining. There were no permissive subjects of bargaining as there are under the NLRA and most state bargaining laws.

To refuse to bargain on just one item and be prepared to defend that position legally would require 10-20 hours of attorney time. Inasmuch as there were no PERB decisions on the scope of bargaining to use as guides, the attorney would have to review relevant cases under the NLRA and the other state bargaining laws very intensively. The discussions at the bargaining table (available in extensive notes by a first-rate secretary) would also have to be reviewed, as would pertinent provisions of the state's Education Code, judicial decisions, and the rules and regulations of the PERB.

Let us see what the litigation would entail. The district would refuse to bargain on the 19 proposals; hence the union would file charges against the district for refusing to bargain on matters within the scope of bargaining. A hearing officer would hear the case and make a recommendation to the PERB. Unless one of the parties filed exceptions, these recommendations would be binding on the parties. Presumably the district would win some and lose some. Assume that it would appeal the losers to the PERB itself. This should not cost a great deal more because the essential argument should have been in the brief before the hearing officer, but there is no way to be sure. In any event, the same considerations apply to the union; it would be likely to appeal the adverse (to it) recommendations of the hearing officer.

When would the hearing officer have a proposed decision? Nobody knows. There is no track record. At this point, the school board has no idea of who the hearing officer will be or how long it will take to get a decision. Also it cannot be sure of the remedy that will be imposed if the union should prevail on some of the issues, as it is likely to do when so many are involved.

Let us assume adverse decisions by the PERB on some items. The district can appeal these decisions to the courts without too much additional costs since the brief for the hearing officer and the PERB will include the main argument to the courts. However, the appeal from an adverse PERB decision may go from superior court to the appellate court to the supreme court. At each level, the district would probably have to defend a legal challenge to the previous rulings favoring the district, just as the union will be facing legal challenges by the district to lower level rulings upholding the union. Thus the school board may be litigating all the issues at five different levels: hearing officer, Public Employment Relations Board, superior court, appellate court, and supreme court. Today we would add three levels of the federal judiciary since federal constitutional issues are arguably involved.

Problem: The unions have introduced legislation that would broaden the scope of bargaining. The district might litigate and win—and it would all be for naught if the legislation to broaden the scope were enacted. *Consideration*: If the district bargains on the disputed items with the classified employees, it will have to bargain on them with the teacher union. Therefore, although the legal costs of refusing to bargain on the disputed items would be substantial, they might be offset in part by savings from not bargaining with the teacher union on a large number of items.

Question: Why should only one district have to pay for litigating these issues when they affect every school district in the state? It should not, but neither the state school-board association nor anyone else would agree to share the cost. Thus the board was facing an expenditure of $25-$100,000, depending on several contingencies. After mulling things over, the board decided to refuse to bargain on the disputed items regardless of the legal costs likely to result from such refusal. As expected, the union filed charges of unfair labor practices, based on district refusal to bargain on the disputed items.

Significantly, the set of union proposals that gave rise to this situation had been introduced in hundreds of school districts throughout the state. Many of them were small districts with budgets 1/20 or less the size of the district under discussion. Unlike the latter, which could probably cover the legal costs from its reserves, these smaller districts could not. Legal fees of $100,000 out of a $25-million budget are one thing, and they are quite another out of a budget of $1.5 million or less.

The upshot is this: When faced with an issue that is important statewide, the unions prefer to press it in smaller jurisdictions. Because these jurisdictions are less able to bear the expense of litigation, they are more likely to concede on them to the union. As they do so, the union then bootstraps the concessions into legal and bargaining gains elsewhere. To both the courts and recalcitrant employers, the union says, How can you assert that assignment (or whatever) is outside the scope of bargaining when 50 other jurisdictions in the state have already agreed to proposals on it?

Considerations such as these may help to explain why the union subsequently dropped its charges in the district just discussed and then litigated the issues in a much smaller school district elsewhere in the state.

Another version of the same technique is to get concessions that have no applicability in the contracting jurisdiction but are useful as precedents elsewhere. Suppose a public employer has only one site. In this case, there can be no transfers (that is, changes in site, as distinguished from "reassignments," which are changes in duties at the same site). The union negotiator tries to persuade the district to agree to a transfer clause, saying that it makes the agreement look better and that the district cannot be affected since it cannot have any transfers anyway. So trying to be good guys, the employer representatives agree. Later the union representatives emphasize the frequency of the concession in negotiations where it would be meaningful.

In considering cost factors, one should not lose sight of union structure. The vast majority of local public-sector unions are affiliates of a state organization. The latter is frequently seeking test cases to establish legal and negotiating precedents favorable to the union. Because the issue is important to the union statewide, its choice of test cases will be based on tactical factors such as the likelihood that the public employer will put up a strong legal case. Ordinarily, and unfortunately, public employers do not have an effective mechanism for sharing the costs of such cases on a statewide basis.

In retrospect, it seems surprising that no state bargaining law appears to exclude public employers under a certain size. There are ample legislative precedents for doing so. Civil rights laws and laws relating to occupational health and safety or to retirement regulations frequently are not applicable to private-sector employers under a specified size. Even in the public sector, legislation on a variety of subjects frequently is applicable only to jurisdictions above, below, or within a specified range of size. Nevertheless, about all there is in public-sector bargaining is that the statutes do not apply to bargaining units with only one employee. This exclusion is not in any state law, but some state PERBs have so held. Their reasoning is that it takes more than one to bargain collectively as well as to tango. Also a secret-ballot election cannot be accomplished with only one voter.

Regardless, the costs of public-sector bargaining in small jurisdictions is all out of proportion to the benefits. Because the costs are so relatively high, small jurisdictions go without competent technical help more often. This in turn adds to their vulnerability in bargaining, grievance arbitration, and unfair practices. It also renders them more vulnerable to irresponsible union leadership. Crackpot employees who would be absorbed or smothered in a large union can easily dominate a much smaller bargaining unit.

Exclusion of small public employers from coverage could be accompanied by a package of statutory protections for excluded employees. This could generate difficult political and legislative problems for public-sector unions since there is no guarantee that they could achieve these protections through bargaining. Unions might nevertheless gain from such an approach. Suppose a bargaining law were blocked in the legislature by rural legislators. If the proposed law did not apply to their constituents, they might be more willing to support it, or at least not struggle so hard to oppose it.

As matters stand, public-sector bargaining is a prime example of the tendency for higher levels of government to impose costs on lower levels without providing any revenues to meet those costs. To my knowledge, only one state bargaining law specifically addressed the question of costs. It does so in a way that is ludicrous, even by state legislative standards. Section 3549(5) of Rodda Act reads as follows: "There are no state-mandated local costs in this act that require reimbursement under Section 2231 of the Revenue and Taxation Code because there are no duties, obligations, or responsibilities imposed on local government by this act." Section 2231 of the California Revenue and Taxation Code requires the state to reimburse local governments for costs incurred in meeting state mandates.

Section 3549(5) is about as absurd as would be a congressional finding that the National Labor Relations Act imposes "no duties, obligations, or responsibilities" on private-sector employers covered by the act. At any rate, let us recall Kerchner's conservative estimate that 1977 bargaining under the Rodda Act cost California school districts $35 million more than their costs under meet-and-confer legislation. The legislative finding that bargaining would not require any additional costs suggests the level of legislative awareness in enacting public-sector-bargaining statutes.[5]

State Costs

Thus far the discussion of costs has dealt solely with those incurred by local public employers. We should not, however, overlook the costs of bargaining to state government. As with local costs, the state costs of public-sector bargaining are diffused through several different budgets. The diffusion is not, however, as extensive as it is for local costs. The reason is that the state usually establishes an agency to administer the state bargaining law. Most of the state costs therefore are normally reflected in the expenses of the state PERBs. In addition to the salaries and expenses of board members, the PERBs employ substantial numbers of attorneys, hearing officers, secretaries, clerks, messengers, and several other positions of varying responsibility.

One major state cost not reflected in PERB budgets is the cost to the state judicial system. State bargaining laws generate a substantial amount of litigation. Data do not seem available on precisely how much, and even if such data were available, it would be difficult to ascertain the costs attributable to the state bargaining laws. Some of the real costs may be obscured beyond hope of identification or clarification. For example, if judges neglect cases because of their workload, created partly by public-sector bargaining, how would one know or compute the costs? Such imponderables are not, however, the major reason why useful cost data are not available. The major reason is the reluctance of the labor-relations community as a whole to address any question that has the potential to jeopardize the enterprise. This reluctance characterizes the management as well as the union side and the impartial third-party industry.

Unions and Union-Member Costs

The costs of public-sector bargaining to unions and public employees are significant issues. After all, we are discussing a representational system for public employees. High costs to employees to participate in that system would be a negative factor in assessing it; conversely, low costs would be a positive factor. We should not force employees to pay heavily for representation that is unlikely to be worth the cost.

What kind of money are we talking about? It was estimated in chapter 1 that public employees pay $750 million annually in local, state, regional, and national union dues. The amounts paid by individual employees vary widely among and between states, local jurisdictions, and types of unions. Most public employees who pay union dues at all probably pay between $100 and $250 a year in dues. Whatever the amounts, they must be distinguished from the costs of bargaining to the individual employees. As we have seen, the division of dues income between bargaining and non-bargaining functions has been the subject of considerable litigation. The litigation typically arises over an agency-shop clause negotiated by the union. Under such a clause, employees in the bargaining unit can be required to pay their share of the costs of bargaining, contract administration, and grievance processing. The costs of these functions is therefore a matter of considerable importance.

From the cases thus far, it appears that most of the dues income (85 percent or more) is spent for bargaining services. Of course, in trying to justify the highest possible agency-shop fee, the unions naturally contend that all their expenditures (legal, public relatons, travel, training, secretarial, and so on) are bargaining costs, directly or indirectly. However, the contrary position has been adequately represented in at least some of these cases, hence the decisions should be reasonably close to the reality.

Because such a high proportion of dues income is allocated to bargaining services, individual employees do not save much by not paying the full amount of dues. The savings are substantial primarily when the employees are relieved of any obligation to pay state, regional, or national dues. This happens where it is held that such dues would go to organizations that are not the exclusive representative and hence have no legitimate claim on the employees for the services they render.

Although unions typically assert that everyone benefits and benefits equally from union representation, it is often easy to identify employees who receive a great deal more than they pay for—and those who receive a great deal less, or may even be worse off as a result of union representation. For most public employees, however, the relationship between the costs and benefits is indeterminate. Inasmuch as the dues level must ordinarily be approved by the membership, or by delegates elected by the membership, we can presume that most union members believe the benefits are worth the dues. Such a presumption would have to be regarded as a rebuttable one since the rank and file is ordinarily exposed only to union communications that support dues increases. These communications typically attribute all the employee benefits to the union; reading them, one would never suspect that any employer had ever provided any benefits apart from the efforts of a militant union.

The Noneconomic Costs of Public-Sector Bargaining

The preceding discussion has been devoted to the economic costs of bargaining. In the author's opinion, these costs are a significant negative factor in public-sector bargaining. We should not, however, ignore the noneconomic costs, which may well be an even more serious objection to public-sector bargaining.

The major noneconomic cost is that public-sector bargaining pollutes our political system. It does so because such bargaining is essentially a political contest. To achieve the maximum gains in bargaining, the union must first create support among its constituents for unrealistic and indefensible objectives. It must then persuade the public that public management is acting nefariously ("not negotiating in good faith"); otherwise, management would make the concessions. More often than not, the attacks on management have absolutely nothing to do with the issues. The strategy is to embarrass or shame public management into concessions as the only way to avoid public criticism, regardless of whether it is related to bargaining issues.

The damage public-sector bargaining does to our political processes has been obscured by some invalid or misleading criticisms of it. For example, collective bargaining does not create the conflict of interest between public employers and public-sector unions. That conflict existed prior to collective bargaining and would exist if there were no bargaining whatsoever. What bargaining does is institutionalize the conflict in several harmful ways.

1. It makes possible and encourages the use of unfair-labor-practice charges as a propaganda tool. Thousands of such charges are filed during bargaining to persuade the community that the public employer is not acting in good faith; the charges are later dropped as part of the contractual settlement or quietly allowed to lapse.
2. It prolongs divisive public conflict through extended impasse procedures.
3. It ritualizes and formalizes employer-employee relations so as to establish a written record for subsequent legal and propaganda efforts.
4. It greatly—even overwhelmingly in many instances—distorts the political process because of the time and resources that must be devoted to bargaining.
5. It fosters posturing as a way of life. In efforts to get more, the union belittles management offers. When agreement is reached on the same offer, however, the union must praise its benefits, inasmuch as it is now the union's agreement too. At the same time management feels constrained to exaggerate its liberality while offering so little that it can improve its offers and not appear inflexible. These postures are not as harmful in the private as they are in the public sector. Public policy should not be made as if it were a battle of wits in some Middle Eastern bazaar.

As suggested previously, it would be intolerable to share governmental authority with other interest groups, as is routinely done under public-sector bargaining. As this is written, government policies are having a disastrous effect on the housing industry. Yet to my knowledge, the housing industry has not suggested that government ought to be legally obligated to engage in bilateral negotiations with builders from which everyone else should be excluded, that it should be an unfair practice for government not to do so, that builders should be able to delay any change in government policy for several months, even for years, if there is no agreement on new policies, or that the differences between government and builders should be submitted to binding arbitration. As R.S. Summers so aptly points out, it is only the tyranny of labels that conceals the negative impact of public-employee unionism on democratic governance.[6]

A Note on Public-Sector Bargaining
as Participation

Despite the absence of hard data on the costs of public-sector bargaining, there is widespread uneasiness about it. After almost two decades of experience with public-sector bargaining, many persons are aware of its tendency to require a substantial amount of public resources.

This widespread uneasiness is frequently rationalized as the inevitable cost of the democratic process. Thus public-employee unions frequently justify public-sector bargaining as a kind of participatory democracy. Public employees frequently have an interest in public policies not only on terms and conditions of employment but on other matters. More important, they have expertise to contribute to the policymaking process. Collective bargaining enables public employees to participate in policymaking in a democratic professional way. Of course, it would be less expensive, at least in the short run, if public officials could establish terms and conditions of public employment by fiat (this is always the sole alternative to public-sector bargaining). Public-sector bargaining ensures that public employees will paricipate in the decisions that affect them. Thus it is the democratic way, well worth whatever the cost over arbitrary, undemocratic ways of public decision making. Thus runs a common bargainist view about the costs of bargaining.

First of all, for most people, participation is a means, not an end. For example, if schools were teaching effectively, pupils were learning, and there were no discipline or dress or behavior problems, most parents would be happy to turn their attention to other matters. Similarly, in the employment arena, if public employees could have a higher salary without participation, they would take it. Of course, the union position is that unless the employees participate, they cannot achieve the objective. But this is a question of fact, which merely emphasizes the point that participation is a means, not an end.

Realistically, if you do not give public employees what they want, they assert that they have not participated—and they never participate enough as long as they do not get what they want. In such cases, the public employer is faking participation. It is not really listening or providing real participation, that is, conceding what the union wants.

Part of the problem is that participation is such a vague term, which means that its disciples can read into it or interpret it in virtually any way they wish. At the same time public employers generally are reluctant to define or circumscribe the phrase; to do so seems like a gratuitous slap at the participants, whoever they may be. In this way, they fall into situations in which they are accused of faking participatory democracy and in which they make concessions as a result of self-inflicted need to legitimize participation.

Whatever may be the value or role of participation elsewhere, there are three major reasons why it is impossible to justify the costs of public-sector bargaining as the price that has to be paid for enhancing participation. The first reason is implicit in the discussion in chapter 4. Even if it be granted that collective bargaining increases participation by public employees in the policymaking process, it unquestionably diminishes participation by others. Conceptually and practically, public-sector bargaining reduces participaton by nonemployees in the formulation and adoption of public personnel policies. Public-sector bargaining is between the public employer and the exclusive representative. On its face, one could hardly expect such negotiations to increase participation by others.

Suppose we were to develop housing policy by bargaining between public agencies and builders. Suppose further that it was illegal (as is ordinarily the case in bargaining with a union) for the public agency to modify the tentative agreements reached in such bargaining. The favored position of the builders would inevitably generate a what's-the-use attitude among others—all the more so because there would be valid reasons for believing participation would be futile. In this connection, the logistics of public-sector bargaining are also conducive to a decrease in participation by nonemployees. There are only so many hours and days available to public employers for getting and considering the views of interested parties. If one devotes enormous amounts of time over several months, sometimes over years, getting the views of the union on public personnel policies, something has to give. And that something, with some exceptions to be discussed shortly, is participation by others.

Participation is diminished, not only for nonemployees but for employees who are not active in the union or are actively opposed to leadership policies. As is the case with nonemployees, the inactive (in the union) public employees or the public employees who do not support the union's policies cannot participate in the policymaking process with the public employer. If they are to "participate," they must do so by becoming active in the union and prevailing there. Whatever may be the merits of this requirement, it is absurd to allege that it increases the participation of the employees who are not active in the union or opposed to its policies. Assume that you are such an employee. Were it not for bargaining, you could attend a city-council meeting and participate in the discussion on public personnel policies. If the number of employees rendered this impractical, you could participate in such a discussion with council members individually. Under bargaining, however, you cannot. Again bear in mind that the Wisconsin Employment Relations Commission and Wisconsin Supreme Court actually ruled that it was an unfair labor practice for the Madison Board of Education merely to listen to a dissident union member speak on a matter subject to bargaining at an open meeting of the board. It is unlikely that bargaining enhances participation when, for all practical purposes, one can participate only by or through internal union activity, and participation directly with the public employer is all but prohibited.

In short, even if it be assumed that participation is desirable and that bargaining increases participation by some, one must look at the total effects of bargaining on participation. The increase in participation by union activists must be weighed against the decrease in participation by nonemployees or employees who lack control or effective access to the operations of the union. On paper, all employees have such access; in reality, the employees who want to change something have to devote their time and resources after working hours to this task. Even if such action were to be successful, the benefits of it are unlikely to be worth the time and effort put in by such employees. Arrayed against them are union officials—full time, with control over union communications. The opposition must pay for its communications out of its own pocket; the incumbents use the union communications, paid from union dues.

As previously noted, there are exceptions to the proposition that participation by nonemployees is reduced as a result of public-sector bargaining. For example, a strike by public employees surely increases participation by everyone. Citizens annoyed or inconvenienced call public officials and write letters to the local paper. The public employees may attend mass meetings, rallies, picket captain meetings, and so on. Whatever else they may be, such activities as slashing tires, blocking ingress and egress to public buildings, cursing employees who do not strike, urging children not to attend school, urging parents not to allow their children in school, appearing in court—all are a form of participation. Apart from a mindless commitment to it, therefore, increased participation is not necessarily socially desirable. Everything depends on the nature of the increased participation.

Another frequent development under bargaining is that there is increased participation on matters subject to bargaining—at enormous cost of participation on other matters. Everyone involved in public-sector bargaining is aware of situations in which the public employer and union have bargained for several months, gone through extended mediation and fact-finding procedures, devoted substantial periods of time to charges of unfair labor practices and court proceedings, met with attorneys and negotiating teams to develop and refine bargaining positions, strategy, and tactics, and perhaps been subjected to a job action of some sort. It can be taken for granted that in this chain of events, participation by just about everyone has increased. But even if increased participation on certain policies were desirable in the abstract, it would not be in practice if it resulted in decreasing participation on other matters. Unquestionably, many communities would be shocked at the enormous amounts of time public employers devote to collective bargaining, and the consequent minimal amount of time devoted to other matters. This is especially true in education, where bargaining has generated strains between teacher unions and parent organizations such as the PTA. Teacher unions typically contend that pupil welfare is their bargaining objective; meanwhile they vigorously oppose any parent or third-party participation in bargaining at the table.

The reality is that although some teacher bargaining objectives such as smaller class size might appeal to parents not deterred by the costs, others would not. In fact, most teacher proposals would eliminate or drastically restrict parent access to teachers and to educational policymaking. For example, teachers often propose that their instructional time be reduced, that they not be required to attend evening meetings (such as PTA meetings or school events), that all parent complaints must be in writing to be considered, and that teachers have the right to have a union representative present when a parent complains about a teacher. It hardly makes sense for a parent organization not to take sides when the issues are of such vital concern to the parents.

Parents feel that they must work with teachers after a labor dispute is over. Unfortunately, the upshot of their neutrality has been to deprive them of most of their influence in bargaining. Realistically, parent interests will frequently conflict with teacher interests as employees. If teachers are going to retaliate against parents, or the children of parents who oppose teacher union policies, parent organizations should confront this problem openly instead of being restricted to neutrality or support for teacher unions.[7]

Reducing the Costs of Public-Sector Bargaining

Regardless of one's views about the desirability of public-sector bargaining, both its economic and noneconomic costs can probably be reduced substantially. Whether they can be reduced sufficiently to render the process acceptable depends, of course, on the nature of one's objections to the process. The direct economic costs to public employers would be easiest to reduce without endangering any legitimate employee rights, but many measures would contribute significantly to a reduction of both economic and noneconomic costs.

Perhaps the most important single remedial action needed to reduce both kinds of costs is to reduce the time devoted to bargaining. As matters stand, public employers are typically required to begin bargaining 90 to 120 days before their budget-adoption date. The rationale was that to be fair to employees, there had to be adequate time not only to bargain but to complete the impasse procedures before the public employer had to adopt a budget for the ensuing year. Unfortunately, this rationale overlooked the dynamics of bargaining. The more distant the deadline for reaching agreement, the less incentive there is for the parties to make concessions. Deadlines far in the future encourage the parties to submit unrealistic proposals since there is plenty of time to modify positions if they are not accepted. Bargaining sessions long before deadlines are frequently reiterations of extreme positions; at this time the alternative to no agreement is simply another session. If the sessions are being conducted on paid time, as often is the case, the employees have an additional reason to drag things out.

The union negotiators are expected to report now and then to their constituents. And so the word goes out—the employer is hard nosed, not bargaining in good faith, has not made any concessions, and so on. The employer is tempted to reply in kind—and often succumbs to the temptation. Also in anticipation of extended impasse procedures, the parties are likely to hold back, anticipating that they will be required to make additional concessions during the impasse period. Inasmuch as the union does not pay for the wasted time, it has no strong incentive to eliminate it. And on the employer's side, the waste may be regrettable, but the taxpayers, not the employer's bargaining team, will pay for it.

Ideally what is needed is the situation suggested by the Italian sociologist, Vilfredo Pareto. Two parties are seated at a table. They have to divide up the coins on the table—but the number of coins is decreasing all the time. In this situation, the parties have to think, and think fast, about optimality, from the perspective of both. We cannot achieve laboratory pure conditions conducive to optimality at the bargaining table, but a different approach to time would be a major improvement. Most experienced negotiators would probably agree (privately, if not publicly) that bargaining against remote deadlines is worse than a waste of time. In fact, it is highly conducive to the worst evils of the bargaining process. It is quite feasible statutorily to telescope the time required and doing so would cause the parties to be much better prepared and inclined to bargain seriously from the outset. The long corrosive buildups by public-sector unions would not necessarily be eliminated inasmuch as the unions could begin to build up the pressure before negotiations began. Still it would be more difficult to launch a campaign against a public employer for refusing to negotiate in good faith before the employer is legally permitted to bargain at all. Furthermore, unfair practice charges would still be available in case a public employer did not live up to its obligations to bargain in the shorter period of time for it. Clearly both parties could be held to higher standards of bargaining conduct if the time for bargaining were substantially reduced.

Finally, although the public-sector unions might publicly oppose a move in this direction, such opposition might be largely pro forma—as pro forma, for example, as might be the support for it from management negotiators. When not employed full time by a public employer, management negotiators tend to be paid by the hour or by the day. On the other hand, the vast majority of full-time union representatives are on salary. They would normally welcome any action that would reduce the time they must devote to individual local unions. For this reason, legislation aimed at reducing the time devoted to bargaining might not meet with all-out union opposition, albeit union support for it is probably not to be expected.

Notes

1. Charles T. Kerchner, "Bargaining Costs in Public Schools: A Preliminary Assessment," *California Public Employee Relations* (June 1979):16-25.

2. Paul F. Gearhart and Richard Krolikowski, "Bargaining Costs and Outcomes in Municipal Labor Relations," to be published in the *Journal of Collective Negotiations in the Public Sector*. The authors agreed not to reveal the communities involved in order to encourage the utmost candor in response to their inquiries.

3. Collective Bargaining and Tenure Study Committee, *Report and Recommendations of the Collective Bargaining and Tenure Study Committee to the Foundation for Oregon Research and Education* (Portland, Or.: Foundation for Oregon Research and Education, 1977). See also the update on the committee report, March 1980, same publisher.

4. See Peter Hennessy, *Schools in Jeopardy: Collective Bargaining in Education* (Toronto, Ontario: McClelland and Stewart, 1979). This book includes an extended discussion of the tremendous noneconomic costs of bargaining; it appears that the dynamics of the process in Ontario are no different from their dynamics in the United States.

5. Kerchner, "Bargaining Costs in Public Schools," p. 16.

6. R.S. Summers, "Public Sector Bargaining Substantially Diminishes Democracy," *Government Union Review* 1 (Winter 1980):22.

7. The Public Education Association in New York City has published some excellent studies of teacher bargaining from the perspective of a parent organization (see bibliography). One study in particular (Silbiger 1980) shows the enormous difficulties confronting third parties under coalition bargaining in New York City, that is, bargaining between the city and

several municipal unions that negotiated as a group through a joint negotiating team. For some case studies and recommendations concerning citizen interest in public-sector labor relations, see Richard P. Schick and Jean J. Couturier, *The Public Interest in Government Labor Relations* (Cambridge, Mass.: Ballinger Publishing, 1977).

8 Concluding Observations

Previously it was suggested that some issues in this study have been largely ignored in the past. To illustrate this point, let us consider briefly the reports that provided the basis for bargaining laws in our two most populous states. The single most influential study of public-sector bargaining in the 1960s was the 1965 *Report of the Governor's Committee on Public Employee Relations*, known widely as the "Taylor Report" after the committee chairman, University of Pennsylvania Professor George W. Taylor.[1] The Taylor Report was the product of five nationally outstanding experts on labor relations appointed by New York Governor Nelson Rockefeller in 1964. All the committee members were neutrals—but they were "neutrals" in a special sense. They were neutrals (arbitrators, mediators, fact-finders) in labor-management disputes, that is, those arising out of collective bargaining. By no stretch of the imagination could any of them be regarded as a neutral with respect to collective bargaining per se.

The Taylor Committee did not discuss the potential conflicts between bargaining and the constitutional rights of public employees; after all, its report was issued six years before the Supreme Court decision in the Sindermann case. Nor did the committee discuss the costs of bargaining or, with one important exception, its impact on the normal processes of representative government, especially the problem of nonemployee or nonunion access to policymaking on matters to be covered by an agreement.

This exception was the relationship between strikes and the political process. The committee was unequivocally opposed to legalizing public-sector strikes. It considered their use alien to our political system and proposed penalties against both individual employees and unions that engaged in a "concerted work stoppage or slowdown . . . for the purpose of inducing or coercing a change in the conditions of their employment."

Despite its opposition to legalizing strikes, the committee failed to recognize the conflict between bargaining and democratic political processes. On the one hand, it recommended that in case of impasse, a dispute between a public employer and public-sector union be submitted to the appropriate legislative body for a hearing. At such hearing, the parties could set forth their positions, including their views on any fact-finding report. After this hearing, the legislative body would be permitted to act. Unfortunately, the provision for a legislative hearing was not based on the potential conflict between public-sector bargaining and the public policymaking process. This is evident from the fact that the legislative hearing was activated only with respect to situations involving an impasse. The Taylor Report did not deal with the exclusion of third parties from policymaking if no impasse had occurred, which is the most frequent situation. Absent a threat to strike, a public-sector union and public employer bilaterally negotiate policies and exclude others in the same political jurisdiction from the policymaking process.

The legislative hearing was a valid idea based on an invalid assumption. The Taylor Committee appeared to assume that government generally, including local government, was divided into executive, legislative, and judicial branches. It was further assumed that the executive branch would do the negotiating and that the agreement would be ratified by the legislative body. Obviously this is unrealistic in the case of many local governments such as school boards. In such governments the executive is not an equal branch but is basically subordinate to the legislative body. Thus in terms of the rationale of the Taylor Committee, the legislative hearing was vulnerable and was in fact repealed insofar as police, firefighters, and teachers are concerned.

Police and firefighter disputes were subjected to binding arbitration in 1974. Also in 1974 the Taylor Act was amended to provide the PERB, not the school board, with an option to conduct a hearing after fact-finding. Subsequently, the PERB held very few legislative hearings. The school board was still free, however, to act unilaterally after completion of the impasse procedures. Technically the change might not have seemed important since it did not affect the employer's right to act unilaterally if no agreement was reached. Psychologically, the change was important since it removed a highly visible confirmation that the legislative process would take precedence in case of a bargaining impasse.

Why was the hearing by the legislative body eliminated only for teachers in 1974? As a result of the merger between the state affiliates of the NEA and AFT in New York, the New York State United Teachers (NYSUT) had become an extremely influential political force in New York, perhaps second to none. NYSUT wanted to get rid of the legislative hearing—and 1974 was a gubernatorial election year in New York. During the gubernatorial campaign, the incumbent Republican governor had said that it offended his sense of justice to have the same legislative body involved in the bargaining also conduct the hearing if and when an impasse occurred. NYSUT effectively exploited this statement. Its weakness is that a legislative body is not a court; the function of a legislative body is to make public policy, not to adjudicate legal disputes. For this reason, the legislative hearing concept was appropriate, despite NYSUT's criticisms of it.

The Taylor Report illustrates the crucial weakness of early analysis of the strike issue. This weakness was the tendency to focus on the effects of strikes instead of their implications for the process of adopting public policies. This misplaced emphasis antedates the Taylor Committee and continues to dominate the literature on the subject.[2] As a result, the professional literature was replete with attempts to compare the consequences of strikes in the two sectors, and to categorize public-sector strikes in various ways that would identify a permissible category. Meanwhile the effects of public-sector strikes and public-sector bargaining on political decision-making were largely ignored.

The major exceptions in the 1960s were the publications (see bibliography) of Harry H. Wellington, Ralph K. Winter, Jr., and Clyde W. Summers; however, their reservations about public-sector bargaining and public-employee strikes were first published in 1969, after public-sector bargaining had been largely institutionalized. Even then their reservations were expressed only as caveats and did not fully delineate the inconsistencies between traditional political processes and negotiating public policies. For example, Wellington and Winter reluctantly supported the legalization of certain kinds of strikes by public employees because of their belief that a total ban would boomerang on public employers who could not enforce it.[3]

Final Report of the Assembly Advisory Council, 1973

Let us turn next to the *Final Report of the Assembly Advisory Council on Public Employee Relations* (California, 15 March 1973).[4]

The council chairman was Dr. Benjamin Aaron, dean of the School of Labor and Industrial Relations at UCLA. Professor Aaron was a nationally known labor arbitrator; he was most certainly not neutral with respect to the desirability of collective bargaining. Similarly, the other members of the committee were bargaining supporters, who were neutral only in the sense that some of them served as impartial third parties in collective-bargaining disputes.

With essentially the same type of committee as drafted the Taylor Report, the Assembly Advisory Council came up with a report that took for granted the desirability of public-sector bargaining. Not a single hard question concerning its desirability was raised in the report. This is understandable; although the assembly did not request the advisory council to propose a bargaining statute per se, it gave the council a list of questions that clearly presupposed council recommendation of a negotiations statute.[5]

Although some important advisory council recommendations were not followed, the report itself clearly played an influential role in California's bargaining statutes. The major recommendations that were *not* enacted were as follows:

1. The council report recommended a comprehensive bill covering all state and local employees; in fact, state employees, local government employees, higher education employees, and school districts are covered by different statutes.
2. The council report recommended legalizing the right to strike; the bargaining statutes are silent on this issue.
3. The council report recommended that bargaining agreements take precedence over any statutes or regulations or ordinances in conflict with the agreements; however, the Rodda Act, which applies to school districts, provides that nothing in the act can be interpreted to supersede the provisions of the Education Code. (This was a recognition of the enormous statutory benefits provided school-district employees—and the political power of the school-district employee unions.) The other bargaining statutes are either silent in the issue or provide that negotiated agreements take precedence over conflicting statutes.

It is especially significant that in recommending a negotiations statute, the advisory council did not even raise, let alone discuss, the following issues.

First, the impact of bargaining on the political process such as the basic issues raised in chapter 4. As a matter of fact, the advisory council simply assumed the subordination of democratic political processes to the requirements of collective bargaining. In recommending that bargaining agreements take precedence over statutes or regulations or ordinances, the advisory council stated:

> Finally, by leaving the initiative to the parties themselves in expanding the scope of bargaining into areas presently covered by other laws, we believe that active publics will be able to exercise a greater influence than before in shaping the future of bilateral relationships in the public sector.
> Regarding the last point, the tendency for labor-management disputes in the public sector to become enmeshed in broader community agencies is well known to the parties. With increasing frequency, such entanglements revolve about what the scope of bilateral determination should be. *By its very nature, bilateral determination in labor relations excludes third-party groups from the decision-making process.* Nevertheless, the efforts of such groups to become involved in community issues affected by collective bargaining will have an impact on the scope of bargaining.[6]

This statement is remarkable, especially in conjunction with the council's express refusal to recommend a management-rights clause or limitations on the scope of bargaining in its recommended statute. In effect, it would give public-sector unions the right to bilateral determination of any public policies that the public employer agreed to have bilaterally determined. Apparently the council had no criterion by which to decide what ought to be bilaterally determined in the public sector; if public management went along, that was good enough for it.

The council also seemed unaware of the basic contradiction inherent in its statement. On the one hand, it was clear that "bilateral determination in labor relations excludes third-party groups from the decision-making process." It then went on to recommend that specific decisions about the scope of bilateral determination be left to such determination. It is difficult to see how this could provide adequate opportunity for third-party groups or why they would "be able to exercise a greater influence than before in shaping the future of bilateral relationship in the public sector." If they are excluded from the process, how would they "exercise a greater influence than before" on it?

Second, the costs of bargaining. The only discussion was whether mediation and fact-finding should be free or whether the parties should pay some of the costs. The council recommended that mediation be provided by the state at no charge and the parties split the costs of the chairman of the fact-finding panel.

Third, the relationship between bargaining and the constitutional rights of public employees. There was no reference whatsoever to the Sindermann case, which was decided about the time the council began its deliberations.

Fourth, the significance of legitimizing strikes from the standpoint of our political processes. In the council's own words, the following considerations dominated its recommendations concerning public-employee strikes:

> First, we sought a prescription that would encourage public employers and employee organizations to reach voluntary settlements or agreements on procedures that they themselves devise for reaching settlements, preferably without third-party intervention, governmental or otherwise.

> Second, we looked for a procedure that would introduce into the psychology of the parties at the bargaining table uncertainty as to the consequences of not reaching agreement, a structure that would make it impossible for either one to predict with accuracy what might happen if the dispute persisted to the point of impasse. We continue to believe that it is desirable to have the parties negotiate in a context of mutual anxiety.

> Finally, we recognized the importance of providing a mechanism for protecting public health or safety if it should be jeopardized.

> With these considerations in mind, we make the following recommendations in respect of a statutory procedure for the resolution of impasses in interests disputes.[7]

The report then went on to recommend mediation and fact-finding, after which public employees would be allowed to strike and public employers would be allowed to lock out employees.

The Aaron Report reflects the tendency in the 1970s to ease the restrictions on public-sector bargaining. The recommendations to legalize strikes and broaden the scope of bargaining illustrate this trend. Bargainists contend that this trend confirms the view that the NLRA is an appropriate model for the public sector; critics assert that the trend simply reflects the growing political influence of public-sector unions.[8] Whichever explanation is correct, the fact is that the 1970s witnessed tendencies to legalize strikes by public employees, to broaden the scope of public-sector bargaining, and to follow private-sector precedents in such sensitive areas as unfair labor practices and organizational security.

In this connection, one must question the common practice of establishing advisory groups on public-employment relations composed completely or dominated by experts on collective bargaining and full-time members of impartial third-party industry. The mistake here—and it was a costly one—was to assume that individuals who are employed as impartial third parties in disputes arising out of collective bargaining are impartial with respect to the desirability of collective bargaining per se in the public sector. Nothing could have been more unrealistic. The vast majority of academic experts who served on advisory committees also moonlighted as mediators, arbitrators, and fact-finders. Asking individuals who provide a specialized service whether they favor a system of employment relations that greatly increases the demand for such a service leaves a great deal to be desired. The issue might not be worth pursuing were it not for the fact that so many advisory groups on public-sector bargaining were dominated by the impartial third-party industry. Such predominance appears to have played a significant role not only in the uncritical acceptance of public-sector bargaining but in the legislative emphasis that was placed on protracted impasse procedures. At any rate, the record is rather clear that an advisory group that is composed of experts on collective bargaining—whether they be representatives of management, unions, or the impartial third party—is not likely to raise any hard questions concerning the desirability of collective bargaining in the public sector. Where this issue arises again—as it will, even in states with bargaining statutes—it would be desirable to have an advisory group not dominated by bargainists, whether they be representatives of management, unions, or the impartial third-party industry.

The Scope of Bargaining in the Public Sector

The absurdity of the bargaining-policy or bargaining-political action dichotomy in the public sector is especially evident in disputes over the scope of negotiations. Typically, such disputes arise when a public employer refuses to bargain on a union proposal, asserting that it is a policy matter, not a term or condition of employment. In such situations, the state PERBs go into their balancing act. They try to weigh the importance of the proposal as a term or condition of employment with its importance to managerial control. If a proposal is deemed an important condition of employment but not crucial to managerial control, it is held to be within the scope of representation. If deemed of minor importance as a condition of employment but critical to managerial control, it is held to be outside the scope of representation. Obviously, there are many borderline cases.

Initially, it should be noted that the distinction between terms and conditions of employment on the one hand and policies on the other is misleading. A distinction that could be made is between policies on terms and conditions of public employment (that is, public personnel policies) and other kinds of policies. To refer to terms and conditions of employment for public employees (whether statutory or contractual) as if they are not public policies leads to serious confusion. To see why, let us examine an issue that frequently arises in public employment. A public employer wishes to require all its employees to live within its geographical boundaries. Its reasons might include any or all of the following:

1. Prevent the erosion of, and/or strengthen, the community's tax base.
2. Strengthen the local economy by spending tax dollars in the community.
3. Provide more job opportunities for local citizens, especially in inner cities where there may be a very inadequate base of private-sector employment.
4. Foster employee understanding of the community and its problems.
5. Increase local support for revenue measures intended to strengthen public services.
6. Reduce community antagonisms to outsiders who receive community revenues as employees but spend them elsewhere.
7. Encourage more community use of public facilities that cannot be operated economically without a larger user base.
8. Reduce absences, late reporting, and early leaving because of commuting problems.

Without necessarily endorsing residency requirements, we can say that all of the preceding could be legitimate reasons for a community to adopt a residency requirement. They are reasons of widespread importance that justify the widest possible input from the community.

Be that as it may, the public-employee unions invariably regard residency requirements as "terms and conditions of employment." This means that they must be negotiated—and with each public-employee union separately. Theoretically, there will come a time (in some jurisdictions) when the public employer can adopt a residency requirement, whether or not the unions agree to it. This would be possible when the impasse procedures are exhausted. Actually, in the growing number of states that have enacted binding arbitration of interest disputes, the public employer may not be able to persuade the arbitrator to adopt a residency requirement (or many others sought by the public employer).

In other words, the public employer has lost its right to adopt a wide range of policies, even if there were unanimous support for them in the community. This hardly seems consistent with the view that public-sector bargaining has no substantive implications. On this score, the bargainist fallacy is to conclude that public-sector bargaining has no substantive implications because it is impossible to predict with certainty any specific substantive outcome of bargaining. Unfortunately, whether bargaining has substantive implications and whether it is possible to predict specific substantive outcomes are two different things.

Consider, for example, the statutes governing elections and political campaigns such as those limiting campaign contributions or governing eligibility for a third party to get on the ballot. One cannot predict with certainty the outcome of any particular election from these statutes. On the other hand, the statutes typically favor incumbents and discourage third parties. Are we to say they have no substantive implications because we cannot predict who will get elected every time? This is illogical, as is the view that public-sector bargaining has no substantive implications merely because we cannot predict the particular content of every contract from a bargaining statute.

Let us add a few additional dimensions. Some states have enacted binding arbitration of interest disputes but only for certain categories of public employees such as police or firefighters. Thus it would be possible for a public employer to adopt a residency requirement for teachers or custodians after completing the impasse procedures with their unions—and be unable to do so for police, firefighters, and prison guards. Or one arbitrator might deny the requirement for one group of public employees while a different arbitrator upholds it for another. Or one arbitrator might deny the requirement one year and a different arbitrator might uphold it in negotiations for the next contract.

Is a residence requirement a public policy affecting the community as a whole, or is it just a term or condition of employment? Interestingly enough, some public-employee groups have successfully lobbied for state laws prohibiting residency requirements. Of course, during these efforts, it was not contended that others should be excluded from the policymaking process. Residence requirements were regarded as political issues, subject to our normal political processes.

There are literally thousands of such legislative enactments that predate public-sector bargaining. In countless situations, public-sector unions have proposed the incorporation of these statutory benefits in the collective agreement. The point is not that public-sector unions are remiss for making these proposals, which are frequently accepted by public employers. It is to illustrate the absurdity of the efforts to distinguish terms and conditions of employment from policy issues, efforts that continue to be taken seriously by public-sector unions, courts and some academic experts on collective bargaining. Another striking example of this absurdity is the situation in which state laws, enacted at the behest of public-sector unions, have mandated agency-shop clauses. Pursuant to such statutes, courts are trying to decide how much of public-sector union dues goes to collective bargaining and how much to other functions such as political activity. In the public sector, this effort is absurd on its face. It seeks to differentiate terms and conditions of employment from political issues whereas the inescapable reality is that statutes on terms and conditions of public employment *are* political issues and inherently so.

We are not yet done with our residency requirement. Suppose that every resident in the community supported it. Suppose also that such support developed after a full and open debate, after which the city council enacted a residency requirement. Subsequently a municipal union requests to bargain on the issue. Must the public employer do so?

Absolutely, under most state bargaining laws. Residency would still be a term or condition of employment on which either party must bargain if requested by the other. None of this would be really debatable under most bargaining statutes, but a recent New York case provides an interesting twist to the issue. Through the initiative process, Troy enacted an ordinance that required firefighter wages to be set at parity with police wages. The city successfully challenged the legality of the ordinance, on the grounds that it interfered with the city's right to bargain on the issue. This challenge would have been equally successful if a union had made it on an ordinance to which the union objected.

If a union proposal is outside the scope of bargaining, the employer may nevertheless be forced to bargain on it. This happens when the employer is required to bargain on the impact of such a proposal on matters within the scope of representation. For example, layoffs may be outside the scope of representation by state law. The public-sector union, however, proposes that employees to be laid off get severance pay—let us say $250 for every year of service. The employer must bargain on severance pay since this is a wage item. Similarly, the union may submit proposals on the order of layoffs and on recall to work. Layoffs are deemed to have an impact on a matter subject to bargaining, that is, wages and hours. In effect, an employer negotiating on layoffs frequently is de facto negotiating on the matter excluded from bargaining. An employer who can lay off but only by paying severance pay may be unable to pay the severance pay. As a result, the employer may lose the right to lay off until the completion of negotiations on the impact.

Finality in Public-Sector Bargaining

In a particularly insightful comment, R.S. Summers has pointed out that the terminology of public-sector bargaining has obscured its impact on democratic governance.[9] This point is especially evident in the emphasis on finality or agreement in public-sector bargaining. We are told over and over again that "the name of the game is a contract" or that impasse procedures lack finality or that strikes should be permitted because they exert pressure on the parties to achieve agreement; that is, finality.

This emphasis is essentially antidemocratic. To be sure, agreement between employer and employees in labor-relations matters is highly desirable. It is not, or at least should not be, the dominant consideration in a system of labor relations, public or private. To subordinate everything to agreement would require that employees have a veto power over basic managerial decisions—in effect, that employees be comanagement. Although there are some proponents of this view, they are certainly not in the mainstream of either organized labor or management in the private sector. And, it should be noted, the employer's legal obligation in both sectors is not to agree but to bargain in good faith.

The analysts of public-sector bargaining who emphasize finality in the sense of reaching mutually acceptable agreements, appear to ignore the political dimension to public-sector bargaining. Prior to public-sector bargaining, finality meant action by the city council or school board or other legislative body accountable to the public. Finality did not mean or imply agreement by a special-interest group with such action. On the contrary, government would clearly be paralyzed if such agreement were normally required. Suppose, for instance, that a city government had to achieve agreement with contractors before it could adopt a housing ordinance; suppose, that is, that it had to undergo mediation, fact-finding, and perhaps even binding arbitration of its differences with contractors. Similarly, suppose that the same procedural requirements applied in other fields: Trucking companies had to agree to street and highway ordinances, restaurants and grocery stores to health ordinances, and so on. Government would be a basket case if special-interest groups had the legal right to hold up government action for a long time because they did not agree with it.

Outside the labor field, therefore, finality does not mean agreement with special-interest groups, and their legal rights to block government action are very limited. Finality means final action by the legislative body, not agreement between it and a special-interest group. In public-sector bargaining, however, the latter is frequently the operational definition of finality. Thus impasse procedures are assessed primarily, if not exclusively, on how effectively they achieve finality. Legislation is frequently recommended on this basis. Reading the professional literature on the subject, one would rarely learn that public-sector unions can, like public employers, sometimes be led by incompetent, irresponsible, and unethical individuals with whom it is practically impossible to reach a reasonable agreement. Failure to reach agreement means that something must be wrong with the bargaining statute or the impasse procedure or the public employer or the impartial third party—but rarely with the public-sector union. Realistically, the omission is indefensible; conceptually, it is essential to legitimize the emphasis upon agreement as the ultimate test of a procedure for resolving public-sector-bargaining disputes, at least without jeopardizing the role of the impartial third-party industry.

Except when interest arbitration prevails, fact-finding is usually the last step in public-sector impasse procedures; typically, the public employer is authorized to act unilaterally if fact-finding has been completed and there is still no agreement. Such fact-finding reflects the vacillation between bargaining and the political process as the appropriate procedure to decide terms and conditions of public employment. Fact-finding is supposed to enable the public to become better informed about a dispute. There would be little point to it apart from the assumption that the dispute is basically a political one. Fact-finding supposedly informs the public of the relevant facts in the dispute, thus enabling informed public opinion to be brought to bear upon the parties.

It is questionable whether this rationale can be taken seriously any longer. Simply being realistic about the role of the facts in political disputes generally is basis enough for a thoroughgoing skepticism concerning fact-finding. And in practice, fact-finding is often a fact-avoiding, fact-obscuring, and fact-mangling process. Given the context in which it occurs, this is only to be expected. Two parties are trying to gain the support of public opinion. They do so by emphasizing facts favorable to their position and ignoring, distorting, or downgrading facts unfavorable to it. The supposition that the public becomes better informed through this process is not simply a fiction. It is precisely the opposite of the most common outcome.

In the typical situation, fact-finding is logically irrelevant to the controversies that give rise to it. To illustrate, consider this issue: Should employees be required to join the union, or pay a service fee to it, as a condition of continued employment? This is frequently a fact-finding issue. What facts and arguments are relevant? The union argument is that everyone benefits from union representation, hence everyone should share in the cost. The public employer denies that everyone benefits and cites some of the cases discussed earlier. The employer emphasizes the fact that particular employees may lose promotions or seniority or even their jobs as a result of specific proposals sought by the union; one cannot realistically contend that such employees benefit from union representation. In fact, the employer may challenge the notion that most employees benefit. According to the union argument, the employees are receiving a salary raise because of the union's efforts; the employer may believe the salary increase would have happened even if there was no union.

Does it matter what other agreements provide? Suppose the employer says: "We weren't at those other bargaining tables. We don't know what was said to justify the proposal or to criticize it. Our reasons may not have been articulated or may not have been persuasive to other public employers, but such facts are essentially irrelevant. We know that most contracts in the state include an agency-shop clause; the point is, however, that the values of this community are more consistent with opposition to an agency-shop clause."

In such a situation, the issue is not factual. It involves the values and priorities that are accorded facts that are not in dispute. In such a situation, there appears to be no point to fact-finding. Even when the issues are genuinely affected by factual considerations, not one citizen in a thousand reads the fact-finding report. When a fact-finding report is issued, the local reporter decides what is important, and this is what citizens read—if there is a newspaper in their community, and if the newspaper publishes something about the report, and if anyone reads it.

Given the fact that the vast majority of reporters have no particular competence in public-sector labor relations, what is published is chancy indeed. If there is a local murder or a foreign crisis or a big football upset, the fact-finding issue may be on a back page or not appear at all. When and if it does appear, it is likely to be the subject of self-serving statements and advertisements by both sides. The idea that citizen understanding of the issues results from this process is an absurdity, nurtured by an impartial third-party industry, which privately is often more skeptical of the process than are my comments about it.

Public-Sector Employment Relations
without Collective Bargaining

What will follow public-sector bargaining? What should replace it? As presumptuous as these questions may appear to be, they are unavoidable if this critique of public-sector bargaining is valid.

As to what will follow public-sector bargaining, a great deal depends on the circumstances of its decline. One scenario would be a Supreme Court decision prohibiting public-sector bargaining as it exists. Most likely, there would be legislative efforts to amend the bargaining laws to take account of the Supreme Court decisions. These efforts could conceivably meet a different fate from state to state.

In the most unlikely scenario, the public employer says, "We just learned that the Supreme Court has declared public sector bargaining unconstitutional, so we aren't going to bargain with you any more. Please close up shop and revert to the status of one interest group among many seeking to affect public policies. Sorry about that." And the union burns all public-sector contracts in a spectacular fire, sends out dismissal notices, and goes into a death rattle.

Agreed, this will not happen. The most important factor in the situation is that public-employee unions exist in force. If the Supreme Court were to declare public-sector bargaining unconstitutional for any reason, the unions would try to amend the bargaining laws to overcome the judicial objections. Thus the parties might have to bargain as before, but it would no longer be an unfair labor practice for a public employer to modify a tentative agreement before ratification. The hope would be that such a change might not impact the process and the outcome very much. This might turn out to be the case, at least in the short run.

What about the conflicts between bargaining and the constitutional rights of public employees? In my opinion, the preservation of such rights undermines or at least weakens the rationale for collective bargaining, but the courts might rule that bargaining could exist as long as it did not violate constitutional rights. In such situations, an employer should not have to bargain on an item on which the union has no discretion to accept less than the constitutional or statutory benefits accorded employees. The unions are fond of saying that bargaining is a fraud when the employer claims practical inability to make concessions on important subjects of bargaining. Surely the process is equally fraudulent to the extent that the union cannot legally make concessions on employer proposals. If a legislature wants to legislate terms and conditions of employment, it should at least avoid, or be required to avoid, legislating minimum terms in the public-sector labor contract.

The cost problem is not a legal one and could be ameliorated immediately. Legislatures could limit the time devoted to bargaining, for example, by providing that bargaining must be conducted within a certain time span (say, 2-4 weeks) after which the public employer has the right to act unilaterally. If unions were required to share the costs of mediation and fact-finding, the resort to these procedures and the prolongation of bargaining as a result would decline precipitously. If mediation is to be provided at state expense, it should be available for only limited periods of time. Contracts might be required to run for a minimum of two years; this would be especially feasible if legislative bodies budgeted for at least a two-year cycle.

The filing of frivolous charges of unfair labor practice could itself be an un-fair practice, subject to penalties. A simple requirement that public employers certify a statement annually (including appropriate categories of expenses) as to their bargaining costs could be helpful.

Whether or not these specific suggestions are feasible, the cost problem should be addressed promptly. Some measures would impact the process more than others. For example, specifying a 2-4-week limit on bargaining would have a much greater impact than requiring public employers to cer-tify costs. Unions would object vigorously to such limitations, just as they would to requirements that they share in the costs of impasse procedures. It should be noted, however, that union leaders might privately support some changes to speed up bargaining while objecting to them publicly.

The immediate problem concerning costs is that the problem is not being articulated; only time will tell what happens when it is. Public-sector unions will undoubtedly react to such data by asserting that they simply confirm the obstinacy of public employers. In other words, the unions will try to cite cost data to force concessions to the union as the way to shorten the bargaining process. Politically, they have no alternative since the costs would otherwise be attributed to union persistence in unreasonable demands.

As emphasized previously, judicial scrutiny of public-sector bargaining is likely to lead to changes in it. Nevertheless, it would be shortsighted to rely on the judicial process as the main vehicle for change. Such change can and should be effectuated legislatively, but to do so demands a different ap-proach by those seeking change.

No one should minimize the difficulties confronting efforts to change state bargaining laws, at least to meet the objections to them discussed in this book. The political effectiveness of public-sector unions is greatly enhanced because a few such unions typically enroll a large membership. Thus at the legislative end, it is relatively easy to coordinate the union posi-tion. Such coordination for hundreds or even thousands of public employers is much more difficult. Nevertheless, critics of public-sector bargaining, at least in many states, could effect significant changes if they devoted more attention to the realities and less to reiterating prebargaining ideological ob-jections to it. How can they convince legislatures that the costs of the process are excessive without some kind of data on the costs? Their attitude seems to be that the legislatures did not need data to get us into this mess. Why should we assume they need data to get us out of it? The question is fair enough. The answer is that ideological arguments not based on data have failed in the past (otherwise, there would be no bargaining law); therefore, it would seem to be time to use arguments based on actual ex-perience under the bargaining statutes.

The fact that some important data may involve an element of judgment does not mean that factual arguments will dissolve in a sea of subjectivity.

The essential point is to change the level of controversy, to convert it insofar as possible to policy issues based on a set of agreed upon—or ir-refutable—facts. If there is disagreement on important factual issues, the disagreement itself can generate the empirical research required to resolve the issue. Currently what we have is a struggle between slogans; the legislatures naturally side with the sloganeers who have the most votes.

Let us imagine the world's two greatest labor negotiators are cast as adversaries negotiating on employee salaries. One represents the city of Boondocks, the other represents Local 999, AFSCME, AFL-CIO. As they negotiate, it becomes clear that each is trying to establish salary criteria that would be beneficial to their client. The city's negotiator is urging the use of other public employers in the county as the comparison group—knowing, of course, that this would lead to acceptance of the city's offer. The union negotiator is urging the use of other cities of the same size as Boon-docks—knowing, of course, that this criterion calls for acceptance of the union's proposal. Each negotiator also knows that her adversary has elsewhere urged the criterion being rejected in Boondocks—because elsewhere, the criteria rejected in Boondocks would have been beneficial to their clients.

Anyway, there they are, knowing that criteria are just part of the game, a rationalization of a position taken because it would help their clients, not because it has any other public-policy rationale or justifica-tion. Each has also calculated the consequences of an all-out struggle to achieve the best possible contract for their principals. The calculations of each show that an all-out battle is not worth the gains for the client. However, being the great negotiators that they are, each also knows that the other negotiator has made the same calculation concerning her strategy. What happens next?

Let us suppose that at this point, the identical thoughts occur to both negotiators: What *should* the employees in Boondocks be paid? Suppose we could put aside all the rationalizations and postures and concerns about our reputation as negotiators. Is there a fair basis for resolving this dispute? The following question occurs to each. (1) Is the board's offer fair because it takes into account community priorities? (2) Or should community priorities be based on what is fair to employees? (3) Or to what extent, if any, is it appropriate for community priorities to take precedence over bargaining ones?

Unfortunately, there are no agreed upon answers to these questions. Partly for this reason we do not, even theoretically, have any commonly agreed on basis for compensating public employees. Perhaps there should be none in a democratic society, which presumably is open to change (and therefore continued conflict) on its policies for compensating public employees.

The Tax Revolt

Public-sector bargaining may or may not be a valid response to the issues that allegedly gave rise to it. Regardless, it appears to exacerbate another problem of growing importance, specifically, the breakdown of conventional ways of assessing and paying for public services. Until we come up with better ways and can justify the costs accordingly, taxpayer revolts will grow in number and intensity. Ways of justifying public expenditures when they were not a major economic factor simply are not good enough when this condition has changed. By generating constant confrontations between public employers and their employees, the public-sector unions are likely to incite and strengthen taxpayer resistance to the tax increases required to meet union demands. The ultimate outcome may be to turn over to the private sector many public services, an outcome that would be a major threat to public-sector unions.

Briefly, let us compare the taxpayer role to the purchaser of goods and services in the private sector. If you spend $100,000 instead of $50,000 for a house, you can recognize the differences—larger rooms, better location, more amenities, and so on. Similarly, if you compare an $8,000 car to a $4,000 car, you can compare the differences—using *Consumers Reports* if necessary. Similarly, for much of what we buy, we have some idea of how it compares to a higher or lower quality product or service—or the means are available for us to do so. In any case, most purchases are individual decisions to make; hence individuals can decide for themselves whether the lack of comparative information is important. Of course, we sometimes pay more and receive less, as when we purchase drugs by brand instead of generic names. Nevertheless, even in these cases, the mistake is avoidable, even if we do not take the time and trouble to avoid it.

Unfortunately, these considerations apply hardly at all to government services. The citizen "buys" a lump of services for his tax dollars. For the most part, he has little or no idea of the costs and benefits of each. Furthermore, it is practically impossible for individuals to solve this problem. The impact of a public service such as education is distributed among many individuals, over a long period of time, and in many different places. As a result, the taxpayer cannot assess public services adequately. The taxpayer's personal experience—if indeed there is any, good or bad—is hardly sufficient evidence on which to base a valid conclusion about the service as a whole.

On the other hand, evidence not based on personal experience is also fragmentary, fortuitous, and oriented to special interests. In some cases, both public management and the public employees involved have a vested interest in obscuring the real costs, for the simple reason that most people would regard them as excessive. In other cases, it is practically impossible to identify or allocate either the real costs or benefits of the service. Frequently the real costs are hidden, not by deliberate design but by the structure of government and unrealistic principles of government accounting. For example, the cost of public education, like that of most public services, is significantly underestimated because it does not reflect the true value of the public property used to carry on the service. If the real value of the property and buildings of school districts were included as an element of the cost—as they should be—we might be shocked at the results in some districts.

At any rate, how much more health, education, transportation, or safety could we get for specified tax increases? The question is not how many more teachers or firefighters or police or librarians could be hired but about the results from a consumption point of view, for example, how much could the city reduce fire loss due to arson, increase literacy, or reduce the time required to respond to calls for emergency assistance, and so on. Except in rare cases, taxpayers have no such data. By the same token, they have no data on what would happen if taxes were reduced. Since they do not know what they are getting for their tax dollars, it is difficult to generate support for tax increases and correspondingly easy to generate support for tax decreases.

Looking at the escalating cost of services whose benefits are not clear, or clearly of little or no benefit, or perceived as of no benefit, it can hardly be deemed irrational to limit or reduce their costs. Public employees believe and argue that the citizenry does not appreciate the value of their services, but this begs the question: How valuable are they? In my own field, for example, if anything is clear, it is that educators have (1) exaggerated the benefits of education, (2) understated the costs of education, and (3) are widely opposed to any meaningful system of accountability.

In the light of the uncertain benefits and the rapidly escalating costs of public services, it is understandable why taxpayers should attack the problem from the cost side. After all, we cannot expect the taxpayers to come up with clear and persuasive data on the benefits. Bargaining and strikes may well succeed in extracting significant concessions in the short run. It would be surprising, however, if these approaches did not stimulate more citizen interest in, and support for, the privatization of public services.

As Wellington and Winter have pointed out, the privatization of public services has many advantages from a labor-relations standpoint. Private-sector employers would have greater flexibility in dealing with labor disputes. They would be less impeded by political considerations, while unions would also gain the advantages, such as a clear-cut right to strike, associated with private-sector employment. As this is written, the uniformed services (police, firefighters, prison guards, and sanitation workers) are threatening a joint strike in New York City. Obviously, whenever public-employee unions believe they can get more this way, they will resort to coalition bargaining and mini-general strikes, or threats thereof. Privatization would greatly decrease these possibilities. The employees would often be part of a company that provides services to several employers; thus contracts would not necessarily coincide with municipal budgets and would not be so directly dependent upon a single do-or-die confrontation with a specific public employer. Government could more effectively serve as an impartial third party in labor disputes when it was not a party directly.

The privatization of public services involves many complex issues that render its widespread development unlikely in the near future. This prediction might be too conservative if an educational voucher plan is successfully implemented, since such an outcome would result in enormous publicity for the concept of privatization. In any event, so long as we obscure the real costs of public services and fail to develop a defensible basis for evaluating their benefits, public-sector bargaining will only exacerbate resistance to higher taxes. The prospect is not a pleasant one for public employees, but they may lose more than they gain by redoubling their bargaining efforts while ignoring the underlying causes of this phenomenon.

Public-Sector Bargaining and Productivity

Taxpayer resistance to public-employee benefits is only one dimension of the larger problem of productivity in the public sector. This problem was not completely ignored in the early debate over public-sector bargaining; proponents sometimes argued that such bargaining would result in greater productivity. In some situations, of course, it does. For instance, in order to pay for increased benefits, management sometimes finds more efficient ways of providing services. And where inefficiencies do not threaten employee benefits, public-sector unions may find it advantageous to publicize them, in order to demonstrate that inefficient management, not greedy unions or employees, is blocking increased benefits.

It is virtually certain, however, that the overall impact of public-sector bargaining on productivity has been negative. The extent obviously varies, but it seems disingenuous to contend that the issue is really in doubt. Again and again, often on a statewide basis, public-sector unions have submitted comprehensive demands that included the following:

1. Less work for more pay.
2. Prohibitions against the contracting out of bargaining-unit work.
3. Prohibitions against hiring nonunit members to perform unit work.

4. Restrictions on the assignment and transfer of unit members, intended to bring about increased efficiencies.
5. Released time with pay for bargaining, processing grievances, union meetings, and union business.
6. Use of public facilities and services for union business, for example, checkoff of union dues at public expense and use of public facilities at no charge for union meetings.
7. Protections against layoffs, including layoffs due to a merger or consolidation that results in employees not being required to perform the work.
8. Costly staffing requirements, such as three-person sanitation crews, two-person patrol cars, and smaller classes.
9. Time-consuming administrative procedures, for example, requirements that management meet with employees and union representatives before taking action on a wide range of actions.
10. Demands for pay for not working or increased pay for not working, for example, pay for layover time and minimum call-in and call-back time.
11. More holidays and increased leave benefits and vacation credit.

Demands such as these are typical, not exceptional. To assert that we do not know the impact of such demands on productivity is somewhat misleading. We do not know the precise overall impact of public-sector bargaining on productivity, but this impact is undoubtedly negative. This would not necessarily invalidate the argument for public-sector bargaining. Arguably, some loss of productivity is justified because of the alleged benefits of public-sector bargaining. A rational judgment as to whether the benefits are worth the loss of productivity depends on what the benefits are as well as what the loss is in productivity. Needless to say, those who take a skeptical view of the benefits do not require much loss in productivity to challenge the desirability of public-sector bargaining. In this connection, there are some reasons for believing that public-sector bargaining has a more negative impact upon productivity than private-sector bargaining has upon private-sector productivity. In the public sector, market constraints do not exist or are less effective; there is less incentive for management to oppose union demands that decrease productivity, especially if, as is often the case, the impact of management concessions on productivity is not evident to the public at large.

On this issue, management statements are often as suspect and as self-serving as union statements. At the outset of bargaining, management often emphasizes the need to eliminate contractual clauses that decrease productivity. Subsequently, however, public management is understandably reluctant to concede publicly that its negotiated contracts will result in decreased productivity. In fact, collusion between public management and public-sector unions to avoid public awareness of the consequences of negotiated agreements constitutes a major problem in developing sound public policy in this area.

The Conclusion Restated

Strong organizations, including strong organizations of public employees, are a social, not just a special, interest. Individuals are typically unable to protect their rights against arbitrary and discriminatory government; hence strong organizations of businessmen, farmers, consumers, and other interest groups generally are desirable. This is a conservative but valid argument for strong organizations of public employees. Therefore, although this study may be interpreted as an attack on strong organizations of public employees, it is not such an attack and should not be so interpreted. Instead, it is a criticism of a specific kind of organization, with specific rights and privileges. At the risk of oversimplification, the public-sector union is a hybrid union-political party, with most of the advantages of both and most of the disadvantages of neither. It would be desirable to have a new organizational structure to replace public-sector unionism, but such a structure is not required to justify deunionizing public employment. All things considered, the conventional ways of resolving public-sector labor disputes prior to public-sector bargaining were better for our society. Some were much better than others, and some were hardly defensible, but overall, they were not as harmful. In any event, there is no justification for waiting until something better than public-sector bargaining comes along. It was here and left. The more a new structure is consistent with democratic political processes, the more it will be unacceptable to public-sector unions anyway. The choice is not between public-sector bargaining and something new; it is between public-sector bargaining and something better. Without in any way idealizing what preceded public-sector bargaining, it was better.

Notes

1. *Public Employee Relations Final Report: A Report Prepared by the Governor's Committee on Public Employee Relations* (Albany, N.Y.: State of New York, 1966).

2. For an early example, 10 years before the Taylor Committee report, see Myron Lieberman, "Teachers' Strikes: An Analysis of the Issues," *Harvard Educational Review* 26 (Winter 1956):39-70.

3. See Harry H. Wellington and Ralph K. Winter, Jr., "Structuring Collective Bargaining in Public Employment," *Yale Law Journal* 79 (1970):822-851.

4. Benjamin Aaron, Chairman, Assembly Advisory Council on Public Employee Relations, appointed pursuant to House Resolution 51, adopted 22 June 1972, *Final Report of the Assembly Advisory Council on Public Employee Relations* (Sacramento, Calif.: Speaker of the Assembly, 1973).

5. "Questions for Assembly Advisory Council on Public Employee Relations Hearing," *Final Report*, Appendix C.

6. *Advisory Council Report*, p. 176. Italics added.

7. *Advisory Council Report*, p. 236.

8. See Tim Bornstein, "Legacies of Local Government," Collective Bargaining in the 1970s," *Labor Law Journal* 31 (March 1980):165-173.

9. R.S. Summers, *Public Sector Bargaining and Public Benefit Conferral*, IPE Monograph No. 7 (Ithaca, N.Y.: Institute of Public Employment, Cornell University, 1978).

Bibliography

The following references provide an overview of public-sector bargaining:

Aaron, Benjamin; Grodin, Joseph R.; and Stern, James L. *Public Sector Bargaining: Industrial Relations Research Association Series.* Washington, D.C.: Bureau of National Affairs, 1979.

Bent, Alan Edward, and Reeves, T. Zane. *Collective Bargaining in the Public Sector.* Menlo Park, Calif.: Benjamin/Cummings Publishing, 1978.

Chickering, A. Lawrence, ed. *Public Employee Unions.* Lexington, Mass.: Lexington Books, D.C. Heath, 1976.

Edwards, Harry T.; Clark, Jr., R. Theodore; and Craver, Charles B. *Labor Relations Law in the Public Sector,* 2nd ed. Indianapolis: Bobbs-Merrill, 1979.

Hamermesh, Daniel S., ed. *Labor in the Public and Nonprofit Sectors.* Princeton: Princeton University Press, 1975.

Lewin, David, Horton, Raymond D.; and Kuhn, James W., *Collective Bargaining and Manpower Utilization in Big City Governments.* New York: Universe Books, 1979.

Loewenberg, J. Joseph, and Moskow, Michael H. *Collective Bargaining in Government.* Englewood Cliffs, N.J.: Prentice-Hall, 1972.

Public Employment Relations Services, *Portrait of a Process: Collective Negotiations in Public Employment.* Fort Washington, Penn.: Labor Relations Press, 1979.

Spero, Sterling D., and Capozzola, John M. *The Urban Community and Its Unionized Bureaucracies.* New York: Dunellen Publishing, 1972.

Chapter 1

Bornstein, Tim. "Legacies of Local Government, Collective Bargaining in the 1970's. *Labor Law Journal* 31 (March 1980):165-173.

Hennessy, Peter. *Schools in Jeopardy.* Toronto, Ontario: McClelland and Stewart, Ltd., 1979.

Public Employment Relations Services. *Portrait of a Process: Collective Negotiations in Public Employment.* Fort Washington, Penn.: Labor Relations Press, 1979.

Ross, Philip. *The Government as a Source of Union Power.* Providence: Brown University Press, 1965.

U.S. Department of Labor, Bureau of Labor Statistics. *Collective Bargaining Agreements for Police and Firefighters,* Bulletin 1885. Washington, D.C.: U.S. Government Printing Office, 1976.

_____ . *Directory of National Unions and Employee Associations*, Bulletin 2044. Washington, D.C.: U.S. Government Printing Office, 1979.

_____ . *Collective Bargaining Agreements for State and County Government Employees*, Bulletin 1920. Washington, D.C.: U.S. Government Printing Office, 1976.

_____ . *Summary of Public Sector Labor Relations Policies.* Washington, D.C.: U.S. Government Printing Office, 1979.

Chapter 2

Burton, Jr., John F., *Public Sector Strikes: Legal, Ethical and Practical Considerations.* Reprint Series No. 448. Ithaca: New York State School of Industrial and Labor Relations, Cornell University, 1978.

Governor's Committee on Public Employee Relations. *Final Report.* Albany: State of New York, 31 March 1966.

Lieberman, Myron, and Moskow, Michael H. *Collective Negotiations for Teachers.* Chicago: Rand McNally, 1966.

Lieberman, Myron. *Education as a Profession.* Englewood Cliffs, N.J.: Prentice-Hall, 1956.

Public Service Research Council. *Public Sector Bargaining and Strikes.* Vienna, Va.: Public Service Research Council, 1980.

Stinnett, T.M. *Turmoil in Teaching.* New York: MacMillan, 1968.

U.S. Department of Labor, Bureau of Labor Statistics. *Work Stoppages in Government,* 1977, Report 554. Washington, D.C.: U.S. Government Printing Office, 1979.

Wellington, Harry H., and Winter, Ralph K. "Structuring Collective Bargaining in Public Employment." *Yale Law Journal* 79 (1970):805-870.

_____ . *The Unions and the Cities.* Washington, D.C.: Brookings Institution, 1971.

Chapter 3

Lawyers Committee for Civil Rights under Law. *State Legal Standards for the Provision of Education.* Washington, D.C.: National Institute of Education, Department of Health, Education and Welfare, 1978.

Schramm, Leroy H. "The Job Rights of Strikers in the Public Sector." *Industrial and Labor Relations Review* 31 (April 1978):322-335.

Stieber, Jack, and Wolkinson, Benjamin W., "Fact-finding Viewed by Fact-finders: The Michigan Experience." *Labor Law Journal* 28 (February 1977):89-101.

U.S. Department of Labor, Labor-Management Services Administration. *Understanding Fact-Finding and Arbitration in the Public Sector.* Washington, D.C.: U.S. Government Printing Office, 1974.

Chapter 4

Cohen, Sanford, "Does Public Employee Unionism Diminish Democracy?" *Industrial and Labor Relations Review* 32 (January 1979):189-195.

Doherty, Robert E., ed. *Public Access: Citizens and Collective Bargaining in the Public Schools.* Ithaca: New York State School of Industrial and Labor Relations, Cornell University, 1979.

Hamer, Irving; Cheng, Charles; and Barron, Melanie. *Opening the Door: Citizen Roles in Educational Collective Bargaining.* Boston: Institute for Responsive Education, 1979.

Miller, Bruce A. "The National Labor Relations Act: Should Amendments Cover Public Employees?" *Labor Law Journal* 30 (October 1979):637-642.

Rubin, Richard S. "The Battle over Residency Requirements: New Approaches by Public Employees." *Employee Relations Law Journal* 4 (no. 2) (1979):257-267.

Summers, Robert S. *Collective Bargaining and Public Benefit Conferral: A Jurisprudential Critique*, IPE Monograph No. 7. Ithaca: New York State School of Industrial and Labor Relations, Cornell University, 1976.

Chapter 5

Bornstein, Tim. "Interest Arbitration in Public Employment: An Arbitrator Views the Process." *Labor Law Journal* 29 (February 1978):77-86.

Pops, Gerald M. *Emergence of the Public Sector Arbitrator.* Lexington, Mass.: Lexington Books, D.C. Heath, 1975.

Staudohar, Paul D. *Grievance Arbitration in Public Employment.* Berkeley: Institute of Industrial Relations, University of California, 1977.

U.S. Department of Labor, Bureau of Labor Statistics. *Grievance and Arbitration Procedures in State and Local Agreements*, Bulletin 1833. Washington, D.C.: U.S. Government Printing Office, 1975.

Chapter 6

Baird, James, and McArthur, Matthew R. "Due Process and Arbitration." In *Bargaining*, ed. Myron Lieberman. Chicago: Teach 'Em, Inc., 1979, pp. 171-178.

Bradley, Philip D. *Constitutional Limits to Union Power*. Washington, D.C.: Council on American Affairs, 1976.

Brief of Public Service Research Council as Amicus Curiae in Support of Petitioners, Pacific Legal Foundation v. Edmund G. Brown, Jr., et al., 3 Civil No. 18364, Third Appellate District, State of California.

Chanin, Robert H., *The United States Constitution and Collective Negotiation in the Public Sector* (May 1971). The author was general counsel and deputy executive secretary, National Education Association.

Gold, Peter. "A Note on the Duty of Fair Representation in the Public Sector." *Journal of Collective Negotiations in the Public Sector* 9 (no. 1) (1980):33-40.

Kahn, Steven C. "Duty of Fair Representation in the Public Sector." *Employee Relations Law Journal* 5 (no. 1) (1979):129-135.

Silber, Richard. "Procedural Due Process: the Skelly Doctrine." *California Public Employee Relations* (June 1980):19-34.

Chapter 7

Institute for Responsive Education. *The Community at the Bargaining Table*. Boston: Institute for Responsive Education, 1975.

Silbiger, Sara L. *Implementing Contracts in New York City*. New York: Public Education Association, 1979.

———. *Coalition Bargaining: Making It Work for New York City*. New York: Public Education Association, 1980.

Chapter 8

Collective Bargaining and Tenure Study Committee. *Collective Bargaining and Tenure in Oregon Education*. Portland: Foundation for Oregon Research and Education, 1977.

Gershenfeld, Walter; Loewenberg, J. Joseph; and Ingster, Bernard. *Scope of Public-Sector Bargaining*. Lexington, Mass.: Lexington Books, D.C. Heath, 1977.

General

The following periodicals are devoted entirely to public-sector labor relations and should be consulted for recent developments.

Arbitration in the Schools. Monthly. American Arbitration Association, 140 W. 51st Street, New York, N.Y. 10020.

Government Employee Relations Report. Weekly. Bureau of National
   Affairs, 1231 25th Street, N.W., Washington, D.C. 20037.
Government Union Critique. Fortnightly. Public Service Research Council,
   8330 Old Courthouse Road, Vienna, Va. 22180.
Government Union Review. Quarterly. Public Service Research Council,
   8330 Old Courthouse Road, Vienna, Va. 22180.
Journal of Collective Negotiations in the Public Sector. Quarterly. Bay-
   wood Publishing Co., 120 Marine Street, Farmingdale, N.Y. 11735.
Labor Arbitration in Government. Monthly. American Arbitration Asso-
   ciation, 140 W. 51st Street, New York, N.Y. 10020.
LMRS Newsletter. Monthly. Labor-Management Relations Service, 1620
   Eye Street, N.W., Washington, D.C. 20006.
Midwest Monitor. Quarterly. School of Public and Environmental Affairs,
   Indiana University, Bloomington, In. 47401.
Journal of Labor Research. Semiannually. Department of Economics,
   George Mason University, Fairfax, Va. 22030.

Private-Sector Collective Bargaining

An extremely comprehensive and lucid summary of the law of collective
   bargaining in the private sector may be found in Robert A. Gorman.
   Basic Test on Labor Law, Unionization and Collective Bargaining. St.
   Paul, Minn.: West Publishing, 1976.
An excellent summary of the structure and dynamics of private sector bar-
   gaining is Beal, Edwin F.; Wickersham, Edward D.; and Kienast,
   Philip. *The Practice of Collective Bargaining,* 4th ed. Homewood, Ill.,
   Richard D. Irwin, 1972.

Indexes

Name Index

Subject Index

About the Author

Myron Lieberman has served as a negotiator or labor-relations representative for public employers or public-employee unions in Arizona, California, Connecticut, Minnesota, New Jersey, New York, and Rhode Island. He has also been an elected delegate to several state and national conventions of public employees and has served frequently as a consultant on a wide range of matters to the American Federation of Teachers and the National Education Association, both of which have commended his leadership in training leaders of teacher organizations on public-policy issues.

Dr. Lieberman received the B.S. in education (1941) and law (1948) from the University of Minnesota, and the M.A. (1950) and Ph.D. (1952) from the University of Illinois. He has taught at the University of Illinois, the University of Oklahoma, Yeshiva University, Rhode Island College, and City University of New York. In addiiton to serving as a distinguished visiting professor at the University of Southern California and the Virginia Consortium on Higher Education, Dr. Lieberman has been a consultant to several state legislative bodies and federal agencies, as well as a number of national organizations. Among his earlier books are *Education as a Profession* (1956); *The Future of Public Education* (1960); *Collective Negotiations for Teachers* (coauthor, 1966); and *Bargaining* (1979).